pc
bv

Break Away

Frances Lincoln Limited
A subsidiary of Quarto Publishing Group UK
74–77 White Lion Street
London N1 9PF
www.quartoknows.com/frances-lincoln

A catalogue record for this book is available
from the British Library.

ISBN 978-0-7112-3808-4

Printed and bound in China

1 2 3 4 5 6 7 8 9

Quarto is the authority on a wide range of topics.

Quarto educates, entertains and enriches the lives of
our readers – enthusiasts and lovers of hands-on living.

www.QuartoKnows.com

Break Away

The heroes and hellraisers
that made road cycling

Euan Ferguson

FRANCES
LINCOLN

Contents

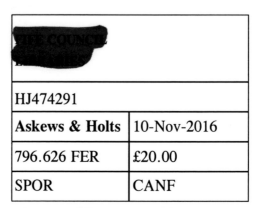

Introduction

"The bicycle is the most civilised conveyance known to man. Other forms of transport grow daily more nightmarish. Only the bicycle remains pure in heart."
Iris Murdoch, in *The Red and the Green*

We could add to the quote above – it's not only the most civilised conveyance, it's the most perfectly designed conveyance. The pinnacle of human invention. Apart from the minor advancements that have been made to its form here and there over the years, it's impossible to improve on. As a mode of transport it's more efficient than the one we were born with.

The bicycle didn't come into being overnight, but it's generally accepted that the earliest evolved from the 'hobby horses' of early nineteenth-century Europe, which in turn took inspiration from the *laufmaschine* ('running machine') invented by Karl Drais in Germany. This was little more than a wooden frame with a seat and wheels – the 'rider' was thrust along by their own feet – but it was better than walking. From there, engineers all over Europe picked up the idea and ran with it, so to speak, and throughout the 1800s the bicycle began to take familiar shape, with steering, brakes and saddles incorporated, and then the component that made it most efficient of all, pedals on cranks. Rubber tyres cushioned wheels, lightweight steel replaced wrought iron. It went from a curiosity to a cutting-edge piece of engineering to a truly democratic new way of moving.

For an delirious but thankfully brief couple of decades bicycle designers responded to a desire for more speed by introducing bigger wheels. Technically

In the 1925 Tour de France, Italy's Ottavio Bottecchia closes in on Lucien Buysse of Belgium. Bottecchia won the tour but died two years later on his bike in mysterious circumstances

speaking this worked, and in the era of the penny-farthing or highwheel, cycling became a faster and much more dangerous hobby. The little-and-large wheel arrangement of these machines (also confusingly known as 'ordinaries') was necessary because power went straight from the cranks to the wheel hubs with no chain to take the strain. Other designs were experimented with, including tricycles and vast lever-driven quadricycles. It wasn't until the idea of affixing a chain between two rings at the pedal cranks and hubs that the aptly named 'safety' bicycle was born and wheels assumed equal size once again; sanity was restored.

The modern bicycle, perhaps made of carbon, aerodynamically corrected, high-tech, is not so far removed from its ancestors in the early twentieth century. The pioneering riders of the first races of the 1900s would be able to operate the machines of today's events with minimal instruction. But although the rate of progression slowed over the last 100 years, the ways the bicycle was used diversified and its story became even more interesting.

Some bicycles are made for dirty mountain tracks, some are for doing tricks, some fold, some go round and round and round on tracks, some can't make their minds up and get called hybrids. But the most unadulterated way to cycle is on the road. Roads go from outside your front door to everywhere. They're laid through forests and fields, beside rivers and oceans. They have hills and flat bits and curves. They don't close when it rains and they're still there if the sun shines. 'Roads were not built for cars,' goes the saying: in the days when the railways seemed to be winning the battle to move us all around, it was cyclists who fought for better surfaces across their countries. Now, commuters and tourers and the pro peloton – all call themselves road cyclists.

The essentially repetitive nature of turning pedals allows the mind to free itself from control, making the bicycle the perfect place on which to focus or just forget. The bicycle allows affordable travel to new places near and far. It's a pursuit for the individualist who wants to get away from everyone else, or the convivialist who seeks company on two wheels. Cyclists are "sociable loners", said the Scottish comedian Billy Connolly. Cycling has long attracted its share of outsiders keen to get even further outside.

The story of road cycling is not just one of transport. It takes in civil rights, the suffrage movement, war, peace, happiness, suffering, nature, politics, love, hate, life and death. More death than you might have hoped for, and more drugs too. For a pursuit that prides itself on delivering its participants fresh air, good health and a happy disposition, too many riders have responded to the demands of a long, hard slog on a bicycle with chemical assistance.

Although most people who take to the saddle do so for reasons of pleasure, leisure or simple necessity, cycles have been used to satisfy our competitive nature since their very invention. It would be impossible to tell the story of road cycling without delving deep into the competition; sport has become the most celebrated form of using a bike. While early illustrious cyclists were pioneers or eccentrics or inventors, for a long time riders of note have been athletes. But in their own way all cyclists are heroic. Look at George Nellis, a reporter from New York state who rode his highwheel to the West Coast in 1887 because it was there and because he could. Or Maurice Garin, who won the inaugural Tour de France in 1903 but was denied his victory the next year because he took a train halfway through. Or Eddy Merckx, the strongest cyclist the world

has ever known, or Marguerite Wilson, who broke records on all-day and all-night cycles in 1940s England, or Nicole Cooke, who wouldn't accept that women couldn't be taken as seriously on a bicycle as men.

This book is an alternative history of road cycling, told through the people who made it what it is today. Because really, it's people who make cycling: without them, bikes are inanimate assemblies of cold parts. Riders make them come alive. But this book *isn't* a hall of fame or a compendium of sports stars. Some of the riders here are winners, some are geniuses, some are superstars, but some are just ordinary people who did something extraordinary on a bicycle. Which we all can do just by getting on and breaking away.

A typical British club run, 1948. Since the earliest days of the bicycle, local clubs have provided informal sociability, exercise and a sense of freedom

Opposite
Henri Pélissier climbs in the Alps between Grenoble and Geneva in the 1914 Tour de France. He came second in that eleventh stage, which involved 325km of riding, and second overall

Next page
The modern peloton climbs Col du Galibier in the seventeenth stage of 2008's Tour de France. The day was won by the Spaniard Carlos Sastre, the eventual GC winner

Kirkpatrick Macmillan

1812-1878

"[His velocipede] appeared to require more labour
than will be compensated for by the increase of speed.
This invention will not supersede the railway."
Glasgow Argus, June 1842

The blacksmith and
amateur bicycle
builder Kirkpatrick
Macmillan with his
children Mary and
John in 1860

The Kirkpatrick Bicycle, 1839

Phantom Bicycle, 1869

Bicyclette, 1879

Kangaroo Bicycle, 1885

Otto Dicycle, 1881

Rudge, 1884

Above
An illustration from *Story of the British Nation, Volume IV*, by Walter Hutchinson, c1923, illustrating the evolution of the bicyle throughout the nineteenth century

Opposite
A late Victorian reproduction of the Kirkpatrick Bicycle held by the Science Museum in London. It looks like a bicycle; it also looks uncomfortable and difficult to ride

Courthill Smithy in the small village in southwest Scotland where Kirkpatrick Macmillan invented his bicycle, 1945

For a machine with such simple principles, the bicycle had a frustrating genesis. There's nothing about its basic parts that an early Victorian with a bit of ingenuity couldn't have built, and yet the first velocipedes were at best awkward, at worst ridiculous. Push-along contraptions, little more than seats on wheels, or oversized wrought-iron cages on wheels. Many of the first human-powered transporters were French (and maybe that's why the French love bicycles so much today), but they seemed to wilfully ignore the basic physics and mechanics that make the modern bicycle such a rapturously uncomplicated piece of engineering.

Kirkpatrick Macmillan was a Scottish blacksmith in the village of Courthill,

Dumfriesshire, and around 1840, in apparent ignorance of earlier versions around Europe, he built the first ever two-wheeled machine that could be driven without feet on the ground. Macmillan's machine had a frame and wheels of wood, like a cart; it was driven by pedals on alternating cranks attached to the rear hub.

He rode it 70 miles to Glasgow, possibly then the longest distance ever undertaken on such a contrivance, whereupon he knocked over a child among a crowd of curious onlookers (the lack of brake may have been a factor). Macmillan was summoned to court and charged, but the sheriff stumped up the five-shilling fine himself, on the condition he would be afforded a demonstration of this remarkable

creation. It was, undoubtedly, a bicycle. Or so the story goes. Like many inventions, the bicycle evolved, rather than appearing fully formed. Several wise men would have liked to be thought of as the originator of this delightful thing. "When an idea is in the air," wrote French cycling journalist Paul de Vivie, "it germinates in many brains."

The Scots are historically an ingenious bunch and like to claim inventions as their own, so let's give Macmillan the benefit of the doubt and add his velocipede to the list along with John Boyd Dunlop's pneumatic tyre, John Loudon McAdam's improved road surface of the 1810s and Alexander Wood's hypodermic syringe: history will record all three as having a profound influence on cycling, for better or worse.

Mark Twain

1835-1910

"Get a bicycle. You will not regret it, if you live."
Mark Twain

Mark Twain, c1865,
takes a more sedate
form of transport
than he would later
adopt when he bought
himself a highwheel.
Alas, no images of
Twain and his bicycle
are known to exist

Riverboat may be the first mode of transport you'd associate with the legendary Missourian penman, but it's less widely known that Mark Twain took to a bicycle late in life, and became a passionate advocate for their benefits. Being the sardonic sort, however, he wasn't reticent concerning their drawbacks and dangers too. For dangerous they were – Twain bought his bike in the early 1880s, when the penny farthing was the ride of the day. In a posthumously published essay, *Taming the Bicycle*, he gives us an idea of how inappropriate the phrase 'it's like riding a bicycle' was. Even getting on these contraptions was a trial.

"You do it in this way: you hop along behind it on your right foot, resting the other on the mounting-peg, and grasping the tiller with your hands. At the word, you rise on the peg, stiffen your left leg, hang your other one around in the air in a general and indefinite way, lean your stomach against the rear of the saddle, and then fall off, maybe on one side, maybe on the other; but you fall off."

By "tiller" Twain means "handlebars", but he really does make steering a bicycle sound as straightforward as steering a steamboat. It took 12 hours of lessons until he felt confident enough to set out alone, and after that many hours of wobbling, crashing, toppling off and huffing and puffing to become halfway competent. He recommends a teacher and 'Pond's Extract' – a treatment for cuts and bruises – as essential investments for the novice.

In plucking up the courage to take to the highwheel and champion the benefits of doing so, Twain was in a minority in 1880s America: bicycles were seen as prohibitively dangerous by most, a passing phenomenon to be enjoyed from a safe distance. Sporadic bicycle booms saw the popularity of riding rise and fall in the US throughout the last 200 years; had his essay been published earlier it might have contributed to one. But as antiquated as Twain's description of his old bicycle may sound, what is still relevant is the freedoms afforded to those who take to the road, and the frisson that the combination of speed and exertion brings. "I started out alone to seek adventures," he writes. "You don't really have to seek them – that is nothing but a phrase – they come to you."

Frances Willard

1839-1898

"Nor could I see a reason in the world why a woman should not ride the silent steed so swift and blithesome."
Frances Willard

Frances Willard
enlists the help of two
assistants as she gets
to grip with 'Gladys',
her trusty bicycle

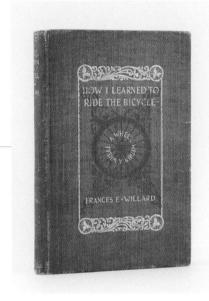

Above left
Frances Willard's book *How I Learned to Ride a Bicycle* urged women to take up riding

Above right
As well as promoting cycling, Willard was a campaigner for women's rights and temperance

Opposite
Female cyclists take to the road in Battersea Park, London, 1895

"Do everything" was Frances Willard's motto, and she gave it a good go. Born in New York state, she was a pioneering suffragist, a reformer, a tireless campaigner for workers' rights and a publisher of educational pamphlets. (She was a fervent supporter of temperance too, but no one's perfect.) She also rode a bicycle, in an era when the very idea of a woman mounting a mechanical contraption in public was a scandal comparable to the exposure of an ankle. Not only did Miss Willard ride a bicycle, she published a book about it, so that women of her day could be inspired and experience the independence that the pursuit provided. *How I Learned to Ride* is inspiring, and full of fascinating descriptions of the practicalities of cycling

in the nineteenth century. "It is needless to say that a bicycling costume was a prerequisite," she writes. "This consisted of a skirt and blouse of tweed, with belt, rolling collar, and loose cravat, the skirt three inches from the ground; a round straw hat, and walking-shoes with gaiters."

Willard estimates that to become proficient on a bicycle takes twenty-two hours' practice, or "less than a single day as the almanac reckons time", as she puts it. Her own cycle she named Gladys; she states she took to it for health reasons, and "to help women to a wider world". The act of climbing on a bicycle was once considered radical, subversive – but the freedoms it brings thanks to the perseverance of pioneers like Willard are universal.

James Moore

1849-1935

"The part that James Moore played in the history of
cycle racing, while of brief duration, was historically of
the greatest importance."
Obituary in *Cycling*, after his death in July 1935

James Moore pictured
in his garden in
Cambridgeshire,
England, in 1930,
with an even-then old
bicycle of the sort he
used to race on

In the Kennington Oval, London, daring chaps attempt some aerodynamic efficiency while pedalling their penny-farthings in an 1874 race

Probably about five minutes after the first human proposed the idea of travelling along on self-propelled wheeled machines, another human proposed the idea of racing them. Competition is in our nature. The oldest recorded bicycle races were seen as novelties – well, travelling along on self-propelled wheeled machines does sound laughable. Riders were billed as 'performers'. Roads were far from smoothly asphalted surfaces, so most of the sport happened in enclosed spaces, although it wasn't long before city-to-city racing began. A lack of the personal entertainments we know today meant that mass spectacle was hugely popular.

And competitive racing has been seen as a commercial opportunity since the first starter's flag was raised. Early French bicycle manufacturers the Olivier brothers organised velocipede races in the western Parisian commune of Saint-Cloud in May 1868. They were classified by wheel size, and one event was won by an Englishman living in France, James Moore: 'The Flying Frenchie' to those over the Channel, 'l'Anglais Volant' in his adopted homeland (he had lived in France since the age of four). For decades he was popularly thought to have been the winner of the first ever cycle race, although scholars have since cast doubt on the validity of this claim, as scholars like to do. Undisputed, however, is the fact that he went on aged twenty to win the first-ever proper organised *road* cycle race on

James Moore won the first proper road race, Paris-Rouen, in 1869; here in 1970 enthusiasts recreate the 123km event on vintage bicycles

17th November 1869: Paris-Rouen, 123km in 10 hours 40 minutes. The former Italian pro Marzio Bruseghin described cycling races as "200 idiots trying to cross a white line"; well, these were the original idiots.

It was reported that several women, including the glamorous-sounding 'Miss America', also took part in this race. The rules were fairly simple – get to Rouen, northwest of the capital – but competitors were not to be pulled by dogs or assisted by sails. Anything else went.

As the century drew to a close, such long events were organised all over Europe, and some are still raced today – Italy's oldest, Milan-Torino, was first held in 1876, and the amateur Léon Houa won the topographical sine wave that is Liège-Bastogne-Liège in its inaugural year, 1892. Vienna-Berlin was contested in 1893, and the back-and-forth of Leipzig-Berlin-Leipzig-Dresden-Leipzig in 1891.

This was the era of dwarf ordinaries and honeymoon sociables, of boneshakers, tricycles and quadricycles. Moore became the planet's preeminent racer of the 'ordinary', or penny-farthing. These mounts look to modern cyclists anything but ordinary: absurd or even, technologically speaking, a step back from the machines with equal-sized wheels of just a few years before. But with the contemporary lack of chains and differential gearing, penny-farthings were the fastest way of riding, and Moore, wearing the regulation stiff woollen shorts and cap, rode it faster than most.

George Nellis

1865-1948

"Oh, the beauties of cycling are surely untold,
There's lots to be written, be written,
A tale to harrow thy soul I'd unfold.
On the beauties that yet are unwritten.
With this wonderful pastime there really is naught
That can safely compare with this heroic sport;
Oh, give me a bicycle, rugged and taut,
With its form most truly I'm smitten."
George Nellis

In 1874, twenty-two-
year-old reporter
George Nellis rode
from New York through
Canada, Michigan,
Indiana, Illinois, Iowa,
Nebraska, Wyoming,
Utah and Nevada
to California on his
Columbia highwheel

In the late nineteenth century, the only spectator sport more popular than cycling in the USA was baseball. Track cycling, that is. Every weekend, hundreds of spectators packed into velodromes to watch high-speed two-wheeled heroics. Road cycling didn't feature much – partly because it's harder to monetise, mainly because American roads were notably poor.

The notion of cycling across the US began to gather speed in the late 1800s, and some of this enthusiasm could be attributed to the efforts of George Nellis. He was a reporter for a local newspaper in Herkimer, New York. In 1887 he endeavoured to cross his huge country on a Columbia Expert highwheel, travelling from his home to San Francisco, California, in seventy-two days. What made this herculean effort so much more than a solo flight of fancy was the fact that Nellis sent back regular dispatches to his newspaper, describing the sometimes grim realities of cycling coast-to-coast on a penny-farthing. Aside from baking sun and vicious dogs, his main chagrin comes from the roads – variously of packed straw, or

deep in mud, or covered in dust. America's love affair with motor vehicles was but a glint in Uncle Sam's eye when Nellis rode across America. But the League of American Wheelmen was established in 1888; in 1894 it launched the Good Roads campaign and took it all the way to the White House. By the time Woodrow Wilson signed the Federal Aid Road Act in 1916, the US was on its way

to having a highway system to be proud of.

The ultimate beneficiaries of these macadamised arteries are not cyclists but drivers. Cycling had its heyday in the US, and It's unlikely it will ever be the arena-packing spectacle it was – not as long as monster truck racing exists – but trailblazers like Nellis paved the way for a country where cycling is a more comfortable experience.

Constant Huret

1870-1951

"On the road of life, there are no signs at junctions."
Constant Huret

Long-distance rider
Constant Huret (at
the very top) sets off
on a 100-mile race in
the Parc des Princes,
Paris, in around 1900

'Constant'. What a great name for a distance cyclist. His nickname was more prosaic: 'Le Boulanger', his humble profession before he took to the bike. His career is of interest for two historically notable reasons. Firstly, he won the 1899 Bordeaux-Paris road race, a frankly preposterous 600km one-day test of endurance that took around 14 hours and was motor-paced for the last half (it returned, without pacing, after a 26-year gap in 2014). One cannot cycle this far on bread alone, but god knows what drove the Baker in 1899. There are a few ultra-recognisable names in the list of Bordeaux-Paris winners over the years – Bobet, Simpson, Anquetil – but it's hard to imagine today's top-tier pros taking it on. Secondly, Huret rode professionally for the Simpson Chain team, and in an advertisement for them was illustrated by Toulouse-Lautrec, a famous post-impressionist on a commercial commission. It's the equivalent of Damien Hirst designing a Team Sky promo, but it's symbolic of the huge popularity in 1890s Paris of this new sport of cycling – every level of society was excited by the action, even the louchest of artistes.

Paul de Vivie

1853-1930

"I still feel that variable gears are only for people over 45. Isn't it better to triumph by the strength of your muscles than by the artifice of a derailleur?"

Henri Desgrange, founder of the Tour de France

There is no sport in which journalists have had more influence than professional road cycling: through mythologising, rhapsodising, sanctifying and exonerating, they've made it into no less than an epic battle of man and machine against nature. Their hands ghost through cyclists' autobiographies, making every win sound more significant, every battle more bloody. One journalist who had both a poetic and practical impact on the pursuit is Paul de Vivie, the self-styled 'Vélocio', a Frenchman who swapped the silk trade for the burgeoning bike trade of the late 1800s and first published *Le Cyclist* periodical in 1887. Few described the spiritual experience of being on a bike better than Vélocio: "The bike is not just a transportation tool, but also a means of emancipation, a weapon of liberation. Free spirit and body of moral concerns, physical diseases of modern life, the glitz, the convention, hypocrisy where appearance is everything, where we seem, but we are nothing."

Mechanically minded riders and companies had been experimenting with the concept of variably geared bicycles for years prior, notably in England, where the likes of Eadie and Sturmey-Archer pressed ahead with the development of the internal hub gear. As with all disruptive technologies, not everyone was on board at first. But De Vivie was obsessed with the idea that gears could make cycling more accessible to the masses – to help them tame the dense miles of French *routes* and *cols* – but also to allow professionals to cycle faster, further, steeper. He favoured the derailleur, which went on to revolutionise road riding. De Vivie was a ceaseless innovator, a trial-and-error tester, a practical inventor who tried just about every method possible for shifting a chain on to different-sized sprockets. Hardware manufacturers followed where he ventured first, the most notable being Cyclo, which created the first commercial derailleur in 1924. Although earlier gear-change systems had been permitted in the Tour de France (including the two-sided hub), it wasn't until 1937 that the organisers allowed derailleurs, although to be fair organisers were rarely in favour of anything that would make it even a fraction more bearable for the competitors.

The journalist, inventor and original 'cyclotouriste' stands with a bike fitted with one of his early gear-change systems. He was a pioneer of variable gears (and it seems of the socks-and-sandals combo)

Tessie Reynolds

1877-1955

"It seems to me that the lady racing cyclist is too much of an innovation to be calmly tolerated by the British public at present."

John Keen, a professional cyclist known as 'the fastest man in the world', 1893

Tessie Reynolds in 1893 in the radical outfit she wore to ride 100 miles from Brighton to London and back

Above left
Reynolds wearing her practical 'rational' cycle gear, in contrast to the formal and restrictive clothing that was conventional at the time

Above right
In 1895, a woman wearing bloomers (easier to cycle in than a skirt) poses next to a 'man's' bicycle. Sexist attitudes to cycling were changing

The global cycling clothing market is now estimated to be worth over $2 billion a year. No estimates are available regarding its worth in 1893, but in the business of what to wear on a bike it was a monumentally exciting year nonetheless. The instigator of hysteria was a sixteen-year-old girl from Brighton on the south coast of England, who shocked the civilised world by cycling from her hometown to London and back, around 100 miles, in eight-and-a-half hours. The date was 11th September, Tessie Reynolds was her name. Not only did she accomplish this feat on a man's bicycle, she did it in what was known as 'rational dress': in other words, a practical outfit. The usual apparel for ladies of the day involved elaborate skirting and corsetry which restricted most

movements beyond stepping out of a carriage. Women did cycle in such outfits, but as can be imagined, pace was sedate. Tessie knew that attempting a century cycle in a frock was out of the question, and she also knew how much of a stir she'd cause doing it in rational dress (in this case, a bifurcated tweed number with plus-four-type pantaloons. Still a long way from a skinsuit).

It can't be underestimated how much of a furore her actions caused. The press was full of stories about it for weeks after. The debate ran: should women cycle in such strikingly masculine attire, and should they even undertake such arduous endeavours at all? The consensus on both points from the male cycling world was a firm 'no'. For a woman, riding so vigorously upon a bicycle

ran the risk of unnecessarily inflaming passions or even shaking one's organs into infecundity. Tessie's clothing was scandalous and provocative, they decided, and actually *discouraged* more women from taking to a bike due to the adverse publicity it received. The letters pages of periodicals were hotbeds of angry correspondence, including one from a Percy Irwin Mortimer in *Cycling*, 14th October 1893, who declared himself "much interested in lady cycling" – sure – but concluded dress must not "rob the fair rider of the respect that is hers".

History has shown us that the hot-and-bothered men of the age were wrong, Tessie and her supporters (for there were many) were right. As 100-mile cycles go, hers was one of the most far-reaching ever.

Just a couple of years after Reynolds's ride, this advertisement for embrocation shows a woman cycling while wearing 'rational dress', apparently with no associated breakdown in social propriety

Marshall 'Major' Taylor

1878-1932

"It is, of course, a degradation for a white man to contest any point with a Negro. It is even worse than that, and becomes an absolute grief and social disaster, when the Negro wins out in the competitions."
Cycling Gazette, 1898

Marshall 'Major' Taylor in 1903. In 1899 he became only the second black man in the world to win a world championships in sport

Left
Taylor overcame
prejudice in the
USA to become the
first African-American
man to win a world
championship
in cycling

Opposite
Taylor's success was
so great he raced all
over the world. Here
he lines up against
Edmond Jacquelin at
the Parc des Princes in
Paris, France, in 1901

The peloton of today, despite the paintbox of high-tech colours resplendent on the bikes and apparel, is an overwhelmingly white place. In the 2015 Tour de France the first ever African team rode, MTN-Qhubeka, and were described as leading the way; they very much were, but imagine how much rockier the road was for a black rider in nineteenth-century America.

Born in Indianapolis into a farming family with eight children, Marshall 'Major' Taylor had it tough, no doubt about it, but as the first African-American to win a World Championship in cycling he beat not just prejudice but all the other riders of his day. His autobiography, proudly but accurately titled *The Fastest Bicycle Rider in the World*, details his many heroic exploits on road and

track (he won the one-mile championship in 1899) and is of equal interest as both a story of an incredible athlete and a historical document. You think taking human growth hormone sounds unpleasant? In Taylor's day, nitroglycerine was administered to keep exhaustion at bay during six-day events where competitors were actually expected to race non-stop for most of the whole six days. Every chapter burns with a measured but insistent anger at the racism he faced on and off the bike, from other riders and from race officials, in the Confederate south and the supposedly more liberal north. At a race meet in St Louis, no hotel would accommodate him, so he had to lodge with a "colored family", as he put it. Some white riders, including

the famous Eddie 'Cannon' Bald, wouldn't race with him. The satirical cartoonists of the press were crude and cruel.

Taylor also refused to compete on a Sunday, as it was against his Christian beliefs. But he won all over the world, as far away as Australia; he earned huge amounts of money from his craft, and appeared never to become disheartened by the incessant focus not on his prowess but his colour. He died poor again in Chicago and was buried in an unmarked grave (although later received a more fitting memorial). "In a word I was a pioneer," he said, "and therefore had to blaze my own trail." Understatement of the sport, although the sport has had few black heroes since: progress faltered when Taylor hung up his bike.

HG Wells

1866-1946

"You're never going to ride that dreadful machine of yours, day after day?" said Miss Howe of the Costume Department.

"I am," said Hoopdriver, as calmly as possible, pulling at the insufficient moustache. "I'm going for a Cycling Tour. Along the South Coast."

"Well, all I hope, Mr Hoopdriver, is that you'll get fine weather," said Miss Howe. "And not come any nasty croppers."

HG Wells, *The Wheels of Chance*

In his 1896 novel *Wheels of Chance*, seminal English author HG Wells describes the travails of the hapless but determined Mr Hoopdriver as he sets off on a rickety bicycle from London to the sea. This draper's assistant is no expert rider and is already covered in bruises from early attempts to master the act. Although by the end of the nineteenth century the diamond-framed safety was common, he uses an older and much harder-to-ride design, which marks him out for ridicule on the roads.

Wells is better known for his pioneering science-fiction works like *The War of the Worlds*, but in *The Wheels of Chance* he goes for comic effect while shining a helpful light on an enduring style of cycling it's easy to overlook. Focusing only on those who race is to miss a whole category of road riders. The Bicycle Touring Club (now the Cyclists' Touring Club) was established in 1878; the journalist Paul de Vivie founded the Fédération Française de Cyclotourisme in 1888 (after coming up with the word 'cyclotouriste' in the first place).

To riders of this era the bicycle offered the opportunity of travel, fresh air, association with likeminded others and the relaxation of social strata. To those who could not afford private transport – most people – this was revolutionary. Wells, a keen socialist and keen cyclist, recognised the potential of this new machine which required no science fiction to make it exciting. Today, there are a billion bicycles in the world.

The novelist HG Wells understood the social significance of mass bike ownership: it gave urban dwellers access to fresh air and open spaces while offering companionship and adventure

Maurice Garin

1871-1957

"I suffered on the road; I was hungry,
I was thirsty, I was sleepy, I suffered,
I cried between Lyon and Marseille."
Maurice Garin

Garin was invited back
to do a lap of honour in
the Parc des Princes,
Paris, at the finish of
the fiftieth Tour de
France, 1953

When the spectacularly named favourite Hippolyte Aucouturier was forced to retire midway through the Tour de France due to stomach problems, the stage was set for Maurice Garin to sweep through and claim victory in this sporting institution's inaugural event. It's a wonder anyone finished that race in 1903, given the amount of chicanery, sabotage and general skulduggery that went on: tacks and glass on the road, violence visited upon competitors by rivals' fans, drafting behind automobiles.

Now, in the twenty-first century, the event is so much more than a race: it's a festival, a phenomenon, a three-week psychology session with the French psyche. It was dreamed up by former professional rider, velodrome owner and newspaper proprietor Henri Desgrange to promote his *L'Auto*; even then it was basically a rip-off of rival organ *Le Petit Journal*'s Paris-Brest-Paris stunt of 1891, which was in turn inspired by *Veloce Sport*'s Bordeaux-Paris earlier in the same year.

The first Tour had a slow start, so to speak. Desgrange struggled to encourage riders to sign up; sixty made it to the starting line. The proto-peloton laboured day and night to reach Lyon, more than 450km, on fixed-gear bikes they were required to maintain themselves. Riding surfaces were in general barely better than farm tracks. That year, the last finisher, Arsène Millocheau, crossed the line almost sixty-five hours after the thirty-two-year-old Garin. Le Tour was, however, a runaway success from the word *partez*. Le Grand Boucle – the Great Loop – is the toughest test of human endurance, but also one big tourist-board advert for France. Hilltop villages, winding alpine roads and those fields of sunflowers – all look better with a blurred pack in front.

Garin had won Paris-Roubaix twice in the previous century and went on to win the 1904 Tour de France too, but he had that title rescinded due to what authorities would only refer to as "irregularities". Some say he boarded a train, the sneaky bastard. Even without the weight of history behind the event, there was no limit to what a rider would do to win.

Opposite above
Garin after winning the inaugural Tour de France in 1903

Above left
Garin photographed in 1890

Opposite
A high-waisted Garin on the fiftieth anniversary of his first Tour de France win

Above right
Garin is presented with flowers after winning Paris-Brest-Paris in 1901

Alfonsina Strada

1891-1957

"But where are you going with your hair in the wind,
With your happy heart and charming smile?
Sooner or later, we will arrive together,
At the finish line of love."
Giovanni d'Anzi and Marcello Marchesi,
from the song *Bellezze in Bicicletta*, written
in honour of Alfonsina Strada

Italian racing cyclist
Alfonsina Strada in the
1920s

Strada in the 1930s.
After disguising herself
as a man to compete
in Italy's biggest race,
she became a national
celebrity

As a young woman
Strada was known as
'The Devil in the Dress'
as she raced around
her home town of
Castelfranco Emilia

Next page
The 1961 Giro d'Italia
passes the Capo
Rizutto in Calabria

Professional road racing is a sport glamorised by journalists but invented by their bosses. Almost all of the famous European events were created to promote various fin-de-siècle newspapers; the Giro d'Italia was dreamed up by the editor of the financially toiling *Gazzetta dello Sport* in 1908 – he had one eye on the success Le Tour had enjoyed since the editor of *L'Auto* had dreamed *that* one up five years earlier. The publication had form – it was behind the Giro di Lombardia (first held in 1905) and Milan-San Remo (1907).

The first Giro was raced by 127 riders in 1909, covering 2,445km over eight stages, starting and finishing in Milan. It was a triumph, with the hacks of *La Gazzetta* using their columns to report the athletic exploits of the godlike participants. In reality, most of the men who took part were poor manual labourers attracted by the prize money; many had no financial or mechanical support and some slept the nights in fields. The stages were exhaustingly long, the roads were unkempt, the bikes rudimental. The inaugural race was won by Luigi Ganna.

In 1924, something happened in the Giro d'Italia that had never happened before and has never happened since. Racer number 72, Alfonsin Strada, was not all he seemed. He was in fact Alfonsina Strada, a farmer's daughter from Emilia and an accomplished cyclist who had already won races across Italy representing her true gender. Given that the song on the previous page was written in her honour in the 1950s, it was clear Alfonsina was unable to disguise her feminine wiles; her deception was rumbled on the starting line, but the organisers put publicity over procedure and let her race anyway. The gender-bending and rule-bending worked – crowds of *tifosi* (Italian cycling fans) lined the route to cheer her along: she became something of a celebrity. Broken handlebars, crashes, punctures and injuries did for her chances of winning but despite falling out of the time limit she was permitted to finish – last, it turned out, but nonetheless ahead of the many men who dropped out. The desire to compete existed, but it's debatable though whether or not Alfonsina had a profound effect on the sport – the first women's Giro wasn't staged till 1988.

Henri & Francis Pélissier

1889-1935 & 1894-1959

"Pélissier does not know how to suffer,
and he will never win the Tour."
Henri Desgrange, founder of the Tour de France,
on Henri, winner of the 1923 Tour de France

"Tout le monde est contre nous [all the world
is against us]."
Francis Pélissier

Francis Pélissier plants
one on his brother
Henri, who has just
won the eleventh stage
of the Tour de France,
Briançon to Geneva, in
1923. Francis finished
second

Above
Henri covers the cobbles in the Metz-Dunkerque stage of the 1923 Tour de France

Right
Henri dons goggles in the Briançon-Geneva stage of the Tour de France, 1923. He went on to win that year

The story of the Pelissier brothers should make everyone grateful they weren't trying to make a living by riding a bicycle in early twentieth-century Europe. When Henri from Auvergne set off on his first *Grand Bouclé* in 1914, it was on its way to becoming the biggest sporting spectacle in the world. But its founder, former pro and newspaperman Henri Desgrange, was maniacally egotistical, and harboured what seemed less a disregard for his participants, more an outright hatred. Some of the competition's early rules were alarming in their severity. Riders could wear what they liked, but were not allowed to discard any item of clothing along the route. Same for broken components – even a buckled wheel had to be carried to the end. No mechanical assistance was to be taken from others, on pain of disqualification. There were split stages across days, dorms to sleep in at night. Desgrange was no fan of derailleurs. So they were banned. Stages were cruelly long, often over 400km, meaning racing through daylight into darkness was required. The riders, barely subsisting on prescribed meals, turned to chemicals.

There were four Pélissier brothers, and three became professional cyclists: the youngest, Charles, was a winner without reaching the heights of the older Henri, same with in-between Francis, but together they produced as successful a dynasty as has ever been seen.

In the 1924 Tour the Pélissier brothers Henri and Francis retired in a show of

Above
Francis on the twelfth stage of the 1923 Tour de France, Geneva to Strasbourg. He finished the race twenty-third overall, almost ten hours behind his brother

Next page
Henri and Robert Jacquinot battle through a Pyrenean pass in 1923

anger at their treatment at the hands of Desgrange, and showed a reporter their stash: "Cocaine for our eyes, chloroform to rub on our gums, pills for strength. We run on dynamite." This journalist, Albert Londres, saw a scoop and filed to *Le Petit Parisien* one of the most famous despatches from cycling, later coining the phrase 'les forçats de la route' to describe riders who took part in these races. 'Forçats' translates to English as something between 'convict', 'labourer' and 'prisoner'.

This situation was the same across all the big races of the day, which existed primarily for promotion of a commercial interest, secondly for the entertainment of the bloodthirsty public. The rights of the largely working-class riders were none.

The Pélissiers were lone voices against this indignity and hardship, and thus did not include Desgrange among their supporters; however, they won races and so had to be allowed to enter. The three brothers were one-day specialists, winning between them several instalments of Bordeaux-Paris, Paris-Tours, Milan-San Remo and the Tour of Flanders, but the finest Pélissier moment was in 1923 when Henri proved his nemesis wrong and *did* win the Tour de France. Desgrange wanted them to suffer, and they did – riders' conditions in the pro peloton may have improved today, but suffering remains. Henri's hardship, incidentally, was not confined to the bicycle. He was killed by a lover using the pistol his wife had used to commit suicide a few years earlier.

In the 1922 Paris-Roubaix, Henri leads with his brother just behind him. Henri had won the race twice before but only managed tenth that year

Opposite bottom

Henri at the 1919 Tour de France. He didn't finish the race, which was won by Firmin Lambot

Right

Francis waits for mechanical support at Paris-Roubaix, 1920. He didn't finish that year; it was won by the Belgian Paul Deman

Below

Francis grinds his way up the Col du Tourmalet, one of French cycling's greatest climbs

Ottavio Bottecchia

1894-1927

"For Bottecchia, to ride is to work, each turn of the pedal is like a blow of the worker's hammer."
Armando Cougnet, quoted in *Pedalare! Pedalare! A History of Italian Cycling*, by John Foot

A familiar scene from another era at the Tour de France: Ottavio Bottecchia rides the gauntlet of fans on the Col du Tourmalet, 1924

Above
Bottecchia tails Jules Buysse in the first stage of the 1926 Tour de France, Evian to Mulhouse

In the first decades of the Tour de France, riders dealt with their own mechanical mishaps. Bottecchia struggles with an inner tube, 1924

Pro cycling is tough, they say. They're right, but so is growing up in poverty in the north of Italy, surviving WWI gas attacks, contracting malaria, working as a cobbler. Compared to that, fifteen hours on an early twentieth-century bicycle over barely finished roads seems like a breeze. Perhaps this occurred to Ottavio Bottecchia, who left a life of war service and hardship in the Veneto to become the first Italian to wear the *maillot jaune* in the Tour de France (1923), then the first to win overall the next year (for good measure, he did it in 1925 too). His story is one of rags to *maglia*, with the attendant riches that victories brought; he was tough as old leather and won difficult races, it seemed, with ease. At the time, cycling was a sport the poor could make their own, and many did. Today, the middle-class fetishisation of road cycling, coupled with the sheer cost of kitting oneself out in race-ready kit with a carbon bike, means it's a poor man's sport no more.

Bottecchia's death is as speculated on as Elvis's. In June 1927, near the village of Peonis, he was found by the side of the road, his bicycle beside him. He had a cracked skull and broken bones, though his bike was was fine. The inquest was inconclusive. Was he, as conspiracists had it, murdered by the fascist government he openly refused to endorse? Did a farmer kill him, believing him to be a grape-thief, as one claimed on his deathbed? Was it a life insurance scam? Did he fall off and hit his head? Debate rages on, but it seems an unfitting memorial.

Bottecchia at a rudimentary feeding zone at the 1924 Tour de France. He won the first stage and kept the yellow jersey all the way to the end

Alfredo Binda

1902-1986

"Elegance, purity, an artist. He was the epitome of beauty in action."
René Vietto, quoted in *Le roi René* by Louis Nucera

An undated picture
of Alfredo Binda, who
won the Giro d'Italia
five times between
1925 and 1933, a
record shared with
Eddy Merckx and
Fausto Coppi

When Alfredo Binda took to his bicycle in the early twentieth century the idea of 'Italy' was still new – in this former land of city states, he spoke in the dialect of Cittiglio in Lombardy, where he was born, and as a teenager he emigrated to the French port of Nice for economic reasons. Like Bartali, like Bottecchia, he came from a poor family.

"The greatest cyclist ever," they called Binda – he could well be the greatest Italian cyclist ever, at least. He was a winner and he won it all – 'all' being Italian events, for he didn't travel well, so to speak. But in races like the Giro d'Italia, Il Lombardia, Milan-San Remo, the World Championships, he left everyone wheezing in his wake, and while he was at it he left behind his life of adversity using the huge sums of money that success brought him, flaunting it on status symbols in the way of the self-made man.

Sport unifies in a way politics rarely can. Italy badly needed unification in the interwar period, and this individualistic, youthful nation looked to solo sports stars rather than teams to provide it. Binda got his face on a stamp, eventually, but he

couldn't be the glue to hold the country together. He looked like a film star but he was never the hero. He cared only for winning: the fact he pursued a career In politics after retiring from the road is telling. He was an active member of the Fascist party: he typified strength, superiority, total domination. *L'uomo nuovo*, war and death and not much else. Cold, robotic, precise.

Not the passionate Italian of romantic imagination. Binda was paid (secretly and handsomely) by organisers *not* to ride the 1930 Giro d'Italia because it was getting boring. No one else could win a stage, let alone the race (he had finished in pink in the previous three; he won five in total). Only in Italy could a bribe of such perversity be made, taken and celebrated.

Gino Bartali

1914-2000

"From snowstorm, water and ice, Bartali rose like a mud-covered angel, wearing under his soaked tunic the precious soul of an exceptional champion."
Jacques Goddet, Tour de France organiser, 1948

Gino Bartali is
carried aloft on fans'
shoulders in Milan
after winning the 1946
Giro d'Italia

Cycling in Europe in the early twentieth century was a sport of the people. The poor people. And in Italy, despite the fact football loomed large as the 'other' national sport, the people loved cycling (the country won the second-ever football World Cup in 1934, when it was host nation). Gino Bartali was born in Florence into a working-class family, and although his mania for bicycles was apparent from an early age, not much about his physicality suggested he'd be cut out for odysseys of endurance. He was a frail boy, picked on by others. His domineering father wouldn't let him enter an organised cycle race until he was seventeen. He was forced to fix rubber from old tyres on to the soles of his battered shoes to protect them on rides.

But from these beginnings a champion emerged. He developed an 'interval' attack style, breaking up charges forward with feints to suggest fatigue before exploding on again. He stood up on the big stage: the Tour de France, twice, either side of World War II; three Giros d'Italia, many, many one-days. He was a hero in Italy – prime minister Alcide de Gasperi telephoned him during the 1948 Tour de France to tell him about the political turmoil back home that threatened to tip the country into civil unrest. A win for Bartali would provide the distraction/pride that could unite Italy, he said. Talk about pressure. He won. (Imagine how good he could have been if he hadn't smoked like Vesuvius, guzzled wine and eaten kilos of meat every day.)

But a younger rival rose to challenge him and split the country afresh, although on (mostly) non-violent terms. Fausto Coppi and Bartali became yin and yang, the devil and angel on the shoulders of the Italian people. Bartali (nicknamed 'the Pious') was devout, Coppi kept quiet his own sceptical beliefs. Bartali was steadily married, Coppi didn't care for such conventions. Bartali was tradition, Coppi was modern. Bartali was human, Coppi was superhuman. The journalist Curzio Malaparte wrote: "Blood flows through Gino's veins, but petrol runs through those of Fausto."

During the 1950s the Tour de France was contested by national and regional rather than trade teams, so the pair ostensibly rode it together, despite their animosity.

Bartali however has a story that reminds us to put sport in its place. The war in Europe disrupted everything – everything except cycling. Sport-mad Mussolini was the Putin of his day, photographed skiing topless. He recognised the importance of mass spectacle to pump up countrywide pride, and his Fascist party organised a sort-of Giro d'Italia in 1942. (In France, a similarly dubious Tour was held by the Vichy regime.) Coppi was captured in service and held as a POW. Bartali, it emerged years later, cycled miles across Italy to courier secret missives among resistance cells – his celebrity meant he could travel unchecked – and he sheltered a Jewish family in his cellar when all around they were being transported to Nazi camps. A hero on and off the bike.

Fausto Coppi

1919-1960

"Ride your bike, ride your bike, ride your bike."
Fausto Coppi

The great Fausto
Coppi recieves the
adoration of fans
at the Parc des
Princes in Paris
following his win
at the 1949 Tour
de France

Rarely has anyone
ridden a bike with such
effortless application
of style. Coppi climbs
solo in the 1949 Tour
de France

He even looks cool
cycling with a giant
bunch of flowers. A
victory lap, 1949

Coppi was idolised
like a film star. A crowd
of fans hope for an
autograph, 1949

It's a rule of cycling – don't ever say, write or even *think* Fausto Coppi's name without 'The Great' in front of it. Otherwise, 'Il Campionissimo' is enough to let everyone know who you're talking about. The Champion of Champions. Born in Piedmont, he raced till WWII stopped him, then he got back on his bike and raced again. How much more could he have done if war hadn't blown those years out of the middle of his career?

Today's peloton is a dayglo-airbrushed blur, but Coppi pedals forever in twitchy black-and-white. He's a film star: James Dean, Marcello Mastroianni. Today's peloton is fine-tuned, calibrated, measured and computed, but Coppi rode with heart. Heart and amphetamine, 'la bomba', when

it wasn't illegal but still dangerous, fuelling day-long races like ten espressos in a row. He wasn't an athlete, he was a gladiator, suffering for the enjoyment of spectators. He was Italian sport symbolic: macho, romantic, honourable, devious, stopping at nothing to win.

The statistics over his pre- and postwar glory years are incredible – five Giro d'Italia wins, three Milan-San Remos, two Tours de France, one World Championships, one Paris-Roubaix, more, more. An all-rounder, on the bike he had the elegance and precision of a *conduttore*; off the bike, even with too-long limbs and an awkward grin, he was urbanity personified. Despite the fact that he was physically fragile as a feather, breaking a whole skeleton's worth

of bones over the years, and succumbing to illnesses.

He was shadowed throughout his career by Gino Bartali: a rival, a teammate, at first equally successful but ultimately overtaken (the two men famously dismounted cycles rather than assist the other at the 1948 World Championships). In a country where the Pope carries more influence than the prime minister, Coppi's scandalous affair with an army captain's wife was more than the masses could take. The pontiff incumbent stepped in to ask Coppi to return to holy matrimony; Coppi, an atheist, ignored him. He was the devil in disguise but today he's a saint in Italy. Death in 1960 by malaria was ignominious but preserved his majesty forever.

Marguerite Wilson

1918-1972

"These are what Miss Wilson regards as the elements of a good style: no wasteful movements; no sliding about on the saddle for instance; a correct position as between seat, pedals and handlebars; a good 'crouch' minimising wind resistance but not pushing the body so far forward that free breathing is diminished or the lookout restricted; and finally, perfect movements in the muscular thrust, starting from the solid drive when the pedal is in the upper position and ending with a lightning, almost imperceptible, ankle flick that carries it past the lower 'dead centre'."

News Chronicle, 3 August 1939, quoted in *Marguerite Wilson: The First Star of Women's Cycling* by William Wilson

The record-breaking
distance cyclist
Marguerite Wilson on
a refuelling break

Margeurite Wilson
pictured in 1948. She
worked as a traffic
clerk in the south of
England to support her
record attempts

Away from the glare and glory of the grand tours and the classics and the monuments, away from the medals and crowds of the Olympics and championships, cyclists find their own ways to shine. Land's End, on the tip of southwest England, to John O'Groats, in the very northeast of Scotland, is 1,000 miles (with a bit of a detour). Riding it is known as 'going end-to-end': long by anyone's standards, especially if you're trying to do it as quickly as possible. On 31 August 1939, the twenty-one-year-old Marguerite Wilson set off from Land's End on her Hercules-branded lightweight. She arrived at John O'Groats a quite incredible three days, twenty-two hours and fifty-two minutes later, in blackout conditions, with Britain now officially at war.

In the middle of the twentieth century, as the sun was blazing down on a golden age of European cycling, the sport in Britain was under a cloud. Organised road racing was strongly disapproved of by authorities, who wanted their highways kept clear for motor vehicles. Time trialling – one woman or man against the clock – was the bread and butter of amateur racing, yet it had to be carried out in clandestine conditions. Early-morning starts, code-named roads, no visible numbers on bikes, inconspicuously black clothing. The best riders had little option but to cross to mainland Europe to race pro. But amateur clubs flourished nonetheless, and it was in one of these – Bournemouth Arrow – that Marguerite Wilson began to show her class. "I became

'a cyclist' in place of 'the girl who had a bicycle'," she said.

Her speciality was long-distance riding, and she had an almost limitless ability to get on a bike and keep going. Eating, resting and sleeping took subordinate places to simply keeping the pedals turning. Wilson loved racing against both men and women, but didn't remain amateur for long – she was the first woman in Britain to be given a race licence by the National Cyclists' Union, and became a professional on a team sponsored by the Hercules Cycle and Motor Company, the supplier of machines to the first British Tour de France team in 1955.

Prior to 1939 Wilson had beaten many distance records in Britain including London to York and Land's End to London.

She was followed by a caravan which included a chef and back-up equipment, but on her bicycle she was on her own, and her achievement was unparalleled. Contemporary pictures show her looking guileless yet powerful, with diva looks that inevitably earned her the nickname 'The Blonde Bombshell'. The 1939 ride generated great publicity for Hercules, which was for a while the biggest cycle manufacturer in the world; it also sponsored Eileen Sheridan, 'the pocket Hercules', who in 1954 would reduce Wilson's Land's End to John O'Groats time by over a day.

But Wilson was the first, and it's easy to imagine the impact that she made as she sped through some small town in buttoned-up, black-and-white Britain.

In an attempt to redress falling sales, the Hercules cycle company sponsored professionals including Wilson, as well as sending the first British team to the Tour de France in 1955

Louison & Jean Bobet

1925-1983 & 1930-

"Bobet is such a human hero that he owes nothing of his victories to the supernatural. They are drawn entirely from terrestrial qualities, amplified by the humanist's raison d'être: the human will! Bobet is a Promethean hero."

"Bobet (Jean). Louison's double is also his negative; he is the great victim of the Tour. He owes to his elder the total sacrifice of his person, 'as a brother'. This racer, ceaselessly demoralised, suffers from a serious infirmity: he thinks."
Roland Barthes, *Mythologies*

The brothers Jean and Louison Bobet during a stage race in Charleville-Mézières, Ardennes, in 1952

Biographies of pro cyclists often take fairly predictable formats. Start with a breathless description of *that* epic, career-defining moment. Rewind to youth, my first bike, how unprepared I was for my first race. How I met my wife/husband, what I really think about this team or that other rider. My view on doping.

However, the great midcentury French cyclist Louison Bobet had in his younger brother Jean an unusually perspicacious observer, and Jean's book *Tomorrow, We Ride* is one of the most dazzling books written about a life on a bike. Jean too was a professional rider, talented to a lesser degree perhaps but never inferior to his brother. It's emphatically not a biography, he states, but more a reflection on his own life,

that of Louison and the existential meaning of their places in the peloton and the world, with pertinent quotes from Hemingway and Victor Hugo. (Well, he is French.) Jean was best placed to pontificate at length upon the career of a cycling superstar. For Louison *was* a superstar: the first man to win three successive Tours de France (1953, '54, '55), a versatile rider who also counted victories at varied events including Paris-Nice, Paris-Roubaix, the Tour of Flanders and the World Championships. He was one of the first to take on a dedicated *soigneur*, Monsieur Le Bert, who administered transcendental massages and helpful pre-race 'tonics' in silver flasks – contents never fully disclosed, but apparently innocent. Jean describes with love the wartorn landscape

Opposite
Jean climbs in Milan-San Remo, 1955. He finished third, ahead of his brother Louison in eleventh

Below
An undated image of Jean. He was as talented at writing as he was at cycling, which he described as "a combination of speed and ease, force and grace. It is pure happiness"

083

of Brittany where the pair grew up, the all-in *communale* village races, the rivalries and language and tactics and rituals of the peloton.

Louison was an anomaly, a champion who cared only for winning, but a generally nervous and distant fellow beset by ill health. He died in 1983 of cancer. "For a long time afterwards, I went riding with his shadow," says Jean. Their story of brotherly love transcends the bicycle.

Jean's own greatest achievement on a bike was probably his Paris-Nice win in 1953. The philosopher Roland Barthes was perhaps harsh when he described Jean as Louison in negative, but it must be difficult trying to follow in the footsteps of a familial superstar (ask Axel Merckx about that).

However, Jean's musings on cycling are victories in themselves. "The divine surprise comes when you discover that beyond enjoyment lies the thrill of *la volupté*," he writes. "The voluptuous pleasure you get from cycling is something else. It exists, because I have experienced it."

Jean retired at 28 and his employment since included teaching French at a university in Scotland, and putting that wonderful grasp of language to use as a journalist. In *Tomorrow, We Ride* Jean remembers 1952, 'The Year of the Remington', when Louison bought an electric razor to make the task of shaving his legs easier. "You may laugh," he writes, "but you are wrong to do so, and I will explain why." It's well worth finding out.

Above
Louison on a lap of honour at the Parc des Princes following his Tour de France win of 1953. The track was used as the finish line for Le Tour until it was demolished in 1960

Opposite
A lean and graceful Louison climbs the Col de Vars in the Gap-Briançon stage of the 1950 Tour de France. He finished third, twenty-two minutes behind winner Ferdy Kübler

Jacques Anquetil

1934-1987

"The bike is a terrible thing that drives you to make excessive efforts, inhuman efforts. It takes a racing cyclist to understand what it means to hurt yourself on a bike."

Jacques Anquetil

Jacques Anquetil, the best stage racer of his day, in 1967

Great artists, great writers, great cyclists: they have an ability to transcend their human flaws. This man from Normandy was great, no doubt about it – the first five-time Tour de France winner, the first to win all three grand tours, a breaker of the Hour Record. He had what the French call *souplesse* – literally suppleness – the ability to take oneself to the limits of physical capability but still look graceful. He was smooth and wore stardom easily. Which all meant his indiscretions could be overlooked by his adoring fans.

Anquetil's somewhat tangled love life can be summed up thus: seduces wife of friend, moves in with her. Has child with her 18-year-old daughter. Deserts this arrangement, begins new one with stepson's ex-wife. Has child with her aged 51.

Add to this an air of superiority, which meant he didn't operate by the same rules as other riders. During the 1967 Tour de France, he wrote articles for *France Dimanche*, in which he expressed dislike for his rival Raymond Poulidor, and openly admitted to performance-enhancing-drug taking and the buying-off of other teams' riders. Races are not won on mineral water, he pointed out; Anquetil was more of a champagne man, in truth, at least off the bike. He was shockingly vocal about doping, more than anyone ever was or has been while still riding; with his arrogance, it meant that outside of his fanbase the French public kept him at an admiring distance. "Je ne fais que suivre ma nature," he said. I am merely following my nature.

Below
In the 1963 Tour de France Anquetil passes a crowd of supporters near Besançon. He won that year, as he did another four times

Opposite
In 1964, a year he also won the Giro, Tour de France victor Anquetil looks haunted but happy on his victory lap with the second-placed Raymond Poulidor

Beryl Burton

1937-1996

"I was not seeking personal adulation, but a little more recognition would not have come amiss. I was a double world champion in an international sport and it might as well have been the ladies' darts final down the local as far as Britain was concerned."
Beryl Burton

If England had a Flanders, it might well be Yorkshire. The inhabitants love cycling, and they also match their Belgian counterparts for characteristic bluntness and lack of respect for ceremony. From this hilly northern county came one of the best all-round cyclists Britain has ever produced: Beryl Burton was untouchable, especially in time trials, where she set records across all the distances. In 1967 she managed a distance in a twelve-hour TT better than the men's record – it took another two years before a man topped it. If you were a female cyclist in 1960s/'70s Britain, you basically had to settle for silver if Burton was riding; she also won the road World Championships twice and the track championips many more times. Women's

cycling wasn't an Olympic sport until the 1980s, or else she'd undoubtedly have picked up medals there too. Her loyal husband Charlie drove her all over England for early-morning starts in her relentless pursuit of records and podium places.

As well as being great cycling country, Yorkshire is also great rhubarb-growing country, and Burton did plenty of that on the side too, back-bent stalk-picking on a farm owned by a clubman. But it wasn't just the rhubarb that left a sour taste in her life: she harboured understandable resentment at the press and sporting organisers who never appreciated what an incredible athlete they had in their midst. She was left out of the British team for the Tour de France Féminin in 1984, only to be called up last

minute due to a withdrawal: she declined so as not to let down her employers at the farm.

Burton remained amateur for her whole career, citing the agricultural work as a factor in her immense fitness. And as well as strength there was that all-encompassing determination that the best riders have. Her daughter Denise became a champion cyclist too and the pair competed against one another; in the 1976 World Championships Denise outsprinted her mother to take gold, and Beryl refused to shake hands on the podium. "I did our sport a disservice in allowing personal acrimony to intervene, and I can only plead that I was not myself at the time," she said. She probably *was* herself, though: for the best, family comes after winning.

The indefatigable Beryl Burton poses in an undated image. She was the most successful female British cyclist ever

Tommy Simpson

1937-1967

"His body ached, his legs grew tired,
but still he would not give in."
Tommy Simpson's epitaph

Tommy Simpson,
wearing the World
Championship stripes
with pride, at the start
of the 1966 Tour de
France in Nancy

Simpson rode for the respected Peugeot team in an era when very few British cyclists went pro on the Continent

Professional cycling eulogises, celebrates, demands suffering. If every cell in your body is not screaming "stop", you're not doing it right. To sacrifice health, sanity or resolve to the road is noble; to sacrifice life is divine. Save for those wilfully risky pursuits that involve extreme heights, depths or speeds, or one-ton bulls, there is no sport that takes more of its participants.

On 13th July 1967, Tommy Simpson collapsed on the upper slopes of Mont Ventoux in the thirteenth stage of the Tour de France after wavering across the road in fearsome heat. His hands had to be prised from the bars of his Peugeot. In his blood was enough alcohol and amphetamines to override any instinct to stop pedalling. He died there on the bleached rocks of the most famous mountain in cycling, under the Provençal sun, four months before his thirtieth birthday. He had been a British pioneer – Olympic and Commonwealth medals on the track, the first Brit to wear the yellow jersey, and a strong classics rider, winning among others the Tour of Flanders, Milan-San Remo and Bordeaux-Paris, a long, long one-day. If you were a cycling-mad English teenager in the 1960s, you didn't have a choice when it came to bedroom-wall adornment – it was a Tommy Simpson poster or nothing.

Tommy Simpson's guilelessly written autobiography is titled *Cycling is My Life*, and cycling was also his death. It was published in 1966, and so ended up covering a lot more of his life than he ever thought it would. The plain prose makes no mention of performance-enhancing substances. It seemed terribly un-British to take drugs, and despite his jauntily upturned cap, Tommy Simpson was British to the core, born in County Durham. "By gum," he writes on one page.

But like most of the contemporary peloton, he knew that chemical advantage was the only way. This was an era when riders' wellbeing came way down the list of authorities' priorities. Drug-taking was unlegislated until Tommy Simpson's death forced its 'regulation'; we all know how well that turned out. But we remember him for his tenacity, his down-to-earth manner, and the way he forced his unremarkable frame to do remarkable things.

Dieter Wiedemann

1941-

"I'd grown up dreaming of the World Championships and the Tour de France, but for my troubles I'd been sent to the Tour of Lower Austria."
Dieter Wiedemann, quoted in *The Race Against the Stasi* by Herbie Sykes

Dieter Wiedemann
pictured in 1965 in the
kit of his West German
professional team,
Torpedo. He raced the
Tour de France with
them two years later

In front of a rousing
image of a hardworking
miner, the Eastern
Bloc Peace Race
passes through
Poland in the 1960s

The USADA report into Lance Armstrong's
US Postal Service Team concluded
it had run the most "sophisticated,
professionalised and successful doping
program that sport has ever seen". Not
quite. The German Democratic Republic's
innocuous-sounding 'State Plan 14:25'
emerged during the Cold War in the 1970s
and ran until the end of communist rule
in the late '80s; it was a government-
sponsored – government-enforced, even
– policy of systematic drugging intended
to turn the closed state into a sporting
superpower. And it worked: at the Olympics
and other amateur international meetings,
the GDR wiped the floor with bigger,
richer and (more importantly) decadently
capitalist countries. By extension, the

Marxist-Leninist project the country's
leaders espoused was shown to be an
unbeatable success. The secret behind
this prowess was a prescription of steroids,
amphetamines and other performance-
enhancing chemicals, much of it
administered without the knowledge of its
often juvenile recipients. As many as 10,000
were estimated to have been doped; many
still live with associated health complaints.

It was against the backdrop of the
politics of the Eastern Bloc and the Cold
War that in 1948 the Peace Race was born –
a stage event between the cities of Warsaw,
Berlin and Prague, initially competed in
by amateurs from sympathetic countries,
and supposedly the hardest non-pro
competition in the world. Western races

like the Tour de France were commercially driven, so at odds with the utopian ideals of communism. The Peace Race was watched by huge crowds and helped build the foundations for a generation of future riders from East, West and unified Germany, which have produced 1997 Tour de France winner Jan Ullrich, 2015 Paris-Roubaix champion John Degenkolb and the great Dietrich Thurau, who shocked the world by holding the yellow jersey for fifteen days in 1977.

The East German cyclist Dieter Wiedemann represented the GDR in the 1962 and '64 Peace Race, becoming a star (although not on the same level as the revered Gustav-Adolf 'Täve'Schur, who won the event twice). Wiedemann's status brought him under surveillance from the Stasi: it was imperative that such a high-profile figure comported himself like a loyal comrade. He did anything but: in 1964, on a training ride before the German qualifying contest for the Tokyo Olympics, Wiedemann took to his bike and absconded. He became persona non grata in the GDR but was granted asylum in the West and went on to ride professionally for the Torpedo team, competing in the 1967 Tour de France. He was right behind Tommy Simpson when he fell from his bike on Mont Ventoux. Wiedemann's desertion was not sports-related: he was enamoured with Sylvia, a West German girl, and had been separated from her by the Wall. He didn't win the Tour de France, but love won and the pair are still together today.

The Peace Race peloton under the no-doubt approving eyes of Marx and Lenin. The event was as much a propaganda tool as giant pictures of the fathers of communism

Eddy Merckx

1945-

"He came at us from every angle, slaughtered every one of us, like some rabid wild man, some barbarian."
Dino Zandegu, winner of the 1967 Tour of Flanders

Eddy Merckx keeps up the speed during the fifth stage of the 1972 Tour de France. He won the stage and the race, his fourth in a row

Above

Merckx's victories earned him the right to lead the peloton. Here he leads the pack in the Tour de France, 1969. He won, of course

Merckx crosses the line to win the World Championships in Switzerland, 1971

When talking about Eddy Merckx, it's best to get the numbers out the way first. Remarkable as they are – an unrivalled 525 wins across grand tours, classics, monuments, championships and criteriums – statistics, figures and tables are an unsatisfactory method of attempting to describe the man. He raced in an era before power data rendered leg force measurable, so we have to go with myth, metaphor and poetry. 'He hated to lose' – of course he did. That's not enough. Cycling fans love a nickname: 'The Shepherd', 'The Warrior', 'The Panther', all are real – they're usually based on journalists' interpretations of the slightly differing ways riders move. Merckx's, 'The Cannibal', is not a pleasant allegory, but it's accurate. He was, by all accounts, a man who saw others as prey. Even those who proved no challenge were chewed up, swallowed, disgorged, ridden over like shit on the road. Outsprint the sprinters, outclimb the climbers, outclass the all-rounders. It's likely that the levelling effect of science in sport means there will never be another like Merckx. Other riders speak of the terror apparent in seeing him over their shoulder. The fact that he looked like he'd kill you on his bike, off his bike, *with* his bike, made losing to him a preferable option. Between 1965 and 1978, the Belgian won just about every major race, and in 1972 ripped the Hour Record into so many pieces it stayed his for decades: when there was no other competitor on the course, Merckx would just beat himself.

A familiar pose: Merckx after winning the Tour de France for the fifth time, July 1974

Roger de Vlaeminck

1947-

"We always turned up to win. Nowadays they treat races like training."
Roger de Vlaeminck

Roger de Vlaeminck
beasts over the *pavés*
of Paris-Roubaix,
well-travelled ground
for him. He won it
four times as well
as numerous other
classics

De Vlaeminck during
the ninth stage of the
Tour de France, 1971

There's a lot of talk of nicknames in this book. In cycling they're part of the kit. Here's one that says 'hard as granite': Monsieur Paris-Roubaix, Roger de Vlaeminck. The classic that gave this archetypal Flandrian his name sums up everything that's sadistic and masochistic and just plain mad about road racing. ('Road' is used in the loosest sense. Paris-Roubaix surfaces are notoriously malevolent.) Held every April, the 'Hell of the North' snakes through flat, foggy farmland in a dark corner of France over 250km of partially cobbled roads known as *pavés*, which are maintained to primitive standards for the sole purpose of this race. The reward at the end of this torment is a communal shower in a cold concrete block.

The idea was dreamed up by the owner of the Roubaix velodrome to promote his remote venue; the first race in 1896 was billed as a warm-up to the established Bordeaux-Paris.

The Sunday of the event is usually rainy, which makes the course muddy, grim and brutally punishing. When it doesn't rain, the course is dusty, grim and brutally punishing. The participants, streaked with dirt, wearing permanently pained expressions, resemble battleworn soldiers trudging along the Western Front. Those lumpy setts underwheel rattle the will out of even the toughest rider. Most of them don't finish, many don't go anywhere near it (Chris Boardman called it a "circus"). Even the ones that do turn up have a love/hate

relationship. "Paris-Roubaix is bullshit," said Bernard Hinault after he came first in 1981. "Paris-Roubaix is a horrible race to ride but the most beautiful one to win," said the 1984 victor Sean Kelly.

De Vlaeminck's Paris-Roubaix record: fourteen starts, thirteen finishes, four wins (equalled only by Tom Boonen in 2012). And De Vlaeminck made it look simple too, gliding over those stretches of monolithic stones like they were freshly asphalted autobahns. He had a mixture of belligerence and hard-punching tenacity that made him a formidable classics rider, with a particular aptitude for the five 'Monuments' of cycling: Paris-Roubaix, the Tour of Flanders, Milan-San Remo, the Tour of Lombardy and Liège-Bastogne-Liège.

The Tour de France gets the headlines and the fame, but the Monuments are for the connoisseurs, carrying with them the whole spectrum of hurt, glory, hills, straights, heat, cold, beauty and devastation in a single day. De Vlaeminck won them all at least once, one of only three people to do so: the others include his compatriot Eddy Merckx. De Vlaeminck never *quite* matched The Cannibal's one-day statistics and didn't get near his Tour record, but he took up the challenge, something few others dared to do. When Merckx was in his pomp, 1968, he approached the young De Vlaeminck with an offer: "Do you want to ride for me next year? Do you want to attempt Roubaix with my team?" The nineteen-year-old De Vlaeminck: "No, I want to ride against you."

De Vlaeminck stays on the wheel of Eddy Merckx in 1973's Paris-Roubaix. Although De Vlaeminck had won the year before, an arm injury meant he couldn't keep the pace and Merckx won after a 44km solo effort

Francesco Moser

1951-

"He was the most macho macho-man
you ever met in your life."
John Eustice, former US road cycling champion

Francesco Moser
on the Col l'Izoard in
the Tour de France,
1975. He won the
classification for
young riders

What drives a road cyclist *off* the road and into the velodrome? Why swap the views, the fresh air, the independence, the climbs and descents (and the gears) for the round-and-round monotony of the track? The answer used to be: money or weather. Big prizes. Roads in the summer, tracks in the winter. But there's something else: the path between the two disciplines is well-worn. "Give me a pursuit world champion and in three years I'll give you back a champion on the road," said the midcentury *directeur sportif* Raymond Louviot. In that era, the giants of the road took to the oval: Coppi, Anquetil and Merckx all made attempts on cycling's oldest record, the Hour, and all broke it. It's beautiful and terrible in its simplicity: ride as far as you can in sixty

minutes. (The benchmark was set in 1893 by Henri Desgrange, who went on to found the Tour de France.) Bradley Wiggins held it from 2015, and Jens Voigt, the oak-thighed German sprinter who won Tour de France and Giro d'Italia stages, made a good fist of it in 2014. There's no one else to blame if the circuit goes wrong, no one else to take the credit if it works. The word used to describe it most often is 'pure'.

Francesco Moser, Lo Sceriffo, did it too. You don't get a handle like 'The Sheriff' without merit, and Moser looked like he could outgun Wayne, Eastwood and Bronson unarmed. When this man from Trentino saddled up he rode like he meant it – he was too stacked to compete in the mountains (although that didn't stop him

claiming first in 1984's Giro d'Italia), but he smashed through the classics of the 1970s, winning among others the Flèche Wallonne, Paris-Roubaix three times and Milan-San Remo. And there was his Hour Record, in 1984, breaking Eddy Merckx's grip on it, on the same high-altitude track in Mexico City the Belgian had ridden twelve years earlier.

Moser's Hour Record lasted nine years, but what makes it notable is not just the human effort (which was allegedly aided by a then-legal blood transfusion) but the technology. It was momentous. Merckx's Hour Record bike is an elegant machine, although with its wire spokes, drop bars and round-tubed steel frame, it looks like something you'd see locked up outside a pub. Merckx wore shorts, woollen top and leather helmet that day in October. 'Aerodynamics' meant keeping your head down. Coppi, by the way, did his Hour on a bike that happened to be lying around at the Velodromo Vigorelli in Milan.

Moser's Hour machine is space-age in comparison. (It's now owned by Bradley Wiggins, who probably never locks it up outside pubs.) It has a steel frame, although aerodynamically designed with curved oval tubing and built with disc wheels and bullhorn handlebars. Merckx drilled his components to save weight, although modern understanding of airflow tells us holes give wind opportunities to interact with the bicycle in a way detrimental to speed. Moser wore a skinsuit and a smooth cap. And he didn't have those Merckx

sideburns dragging him back either. His medical team, which included a young Dr Michele Ferrari (Lance Armstrong's angel of endurance), paid attention to his anaerobic capacity in a tailored training programme, and measured his heartrate throughout.

Since then, the issue of what constitutes acceptable technology has troubled the UCI, which retrospectively demoted a slew of Hour Records to a new category (including Moser's, and mid-'90s efforts from Chris Boardman and Graeme Obree). It's now back to a trinity: human, basic machine, track. But Moser is still rightly proud of his record, and it represents a watershed in road cycling too – the moment that technology equalled physiology in the neverending race to the finish line.

111

Sean Kelly

1956-

"When I was young I believed in the miracles but I grew out of it. Cycling taught me there are no miracles."
Sean Kelly

A typically determined Sean Kelly covered in northern French mud defending his Paris-Roubaix trophy in 1985. He finished third

More than one commentator has described Sean Kelly as a Belgian who happened to be Irish. The bricklayer and farmer's son from County Waterford was certainly possessed of the same sort of head-down shut-up unshakeable perseverance that defined so many resilient Flemish riders over the years. In some ways, too, he's reminiscent of the French and Italians of the first part of the twentieth century – field workers riding hard to get far away from the financial situation they were born into. Cycling is a job. The romance of the sport is most keenly felt by those who don't have to do it professionally.

Kelly is as down-to-earth as anyone who's ever been part of the pro peloton. He could be describing a harvest or a major cycling victory: his tone barely changes.

"It was a great feeling. Winning always is," he wrote in his autobiography *Hunger*. "I thought, 'Feck, I've won a stage of the Tour de France. That's really something.'" He was part of a holy quaternity of superstar Irish cyclists of the era – with Stephen Roche, who won the World Championships, Tour de France and Giro d'Italia in 1987, Martin Earley and Paul Kimmage.

Kelly's teammates at his first pro outfit Flandria included the world champion Freddy Maertens and Marc Demeyer (who had just won Paris-Roubaix but was to die of a heart attack aged 31). Another thing Kelly shared with the Belgians was an aptitude for the classics. These are the one-day races held across the calendar, with many having roots going back to the nineteenth

century. They're seasonal, with characters that reflect the weather: in spring, things kick off with the Milan-San Remo at almost 300km, often accompanied by horrendous weather. In Flanders, where cycling is a religion along with beer, races like E3 Harelbeke and the Ronde Van Vlaanderen send participants up steep cobbled hills; in autumn the season winds down with the evocatively named 'race of the falling leaves', the Giro di Lombardia. They share something in common: they're torturously difficult. They favour *puncheurs*, powerful riders who can handle short, sharp climbs, rough terrain and flat sprints. Everyone wants to win them. The classics lack the glamour of the grand tours, but hardcore fans know that to win one takes something

special, and many riders see them as more prestigious than the big stage races. The five most important have come to be known as 'the Monuments' – the tours of Flanders and Lombardy along with Milan-San Remo, Liège-Bastogne-Liège and the queen of them all, Paris-Roubaix.

"I've heard stories about myself that have been exaggerated to the point where only my name was true," said Kelly, but it's no exaggeration to say that he was ideally suited to the classics and won more than almost anyone. He was deadly in the sprints, strong in the mountains, fearless in descents, he read the tactics like a grandmaster, but what made him a proper rider was indefatigability. Broken bones, dirty rivals, snow, illness – nothing held him

back. He was hard. Not show-off hard, but *hard*. In 1984 he won Paris-Roubaix then Liège-Bastogne-Liège in one week. Add to that three Giros di Lombardia, another Paris-Roubaix, two Milan-San Remos and the often wild Gent-Wevelgem. World's top-rated rider by points for five years. He bagged a win at the Grand Prix des Nations, a top time trial race in France (which had in the past been dominated by Jacques Anquetil and Bernard Hinault). And he wasn't too bad at stage races too, winning Paris-Nice – 'the race to the sun' – seven times in a row from 1982, four Tour de France green jerseys and first overall at 1988's Vuelta à España. Not bad for the bricklayer from Waterford, who kept the romance of cycling alive for a generation of spectators.

Connie Carpenter-Phinney

1957-

"Everybody rides bikes as kids… Some of
us just wanted to go a bit faster."
Connie Carpenter-Phinney

In the inaugural Ride
the Rockies Tour of
Colorado in 1986,
Connie Carpenter-
Phinney climbs the
Independence Pass

If there ever was an all-round athlete, it's Connie Carpenter-Phinney. As well as cycling, the girl from Wisconsin competed at a national level in rowing and speed skating, winning in all three. She was the youngest ever American female Winter Olympian, entering as a speed skater in the 1972 Sapporo Games aged fourteen. But Carpenter-Phinney's story is one of acceptance that still highlights marginalisation. The 1984 Olympic Games in Los Angeles was the first in which women competed on bicycles. Carpenter-Phinney bagged gold, winning the inaugural road race a split second ahead of fellow American Rebecca Twigg.

"Let me tell you what I think of bicycling," said American suffrage campaigner Susan B Anthony. "I think it has done more to emancipate women than anything else in the world." That was in 1896. Although the sport is now entrenched in the Olympics for both men and women, in the pro world the opportunities were limited for decades following that historic win a century later in 1984. In the spiritual home of cycling, France, there's a battle every year to scrape together enough funding for a women's version of the Tour de France, and it's often a pale imitation.

"Cycling as a male-dominated sport has a long way to go," Carpenter-Phinney said in 2014; when the only women in major European races are there to hand over flowers to the stage winners, it's hard to disagree.

Opposite
Carpenter-Phinney celebrates with her Puch team after winning overall at the Coors International Bicycle Classic in Boulder, Colorado, 1982. Jeannie Longo came second

Above
Carpenter-Phinney and Sue Novara-Reber on a training ride in Colorado, 1983

Bernard Hinault

1954-

"As long as I breathe, I attack."
Bernard Hinault

Bernard Hinault
looking pretty relaxed
before the start of the
Coors Classic in San
Francisco, 1986

Above

Greg LeMond (left)
and Hinault cross the
line together in the
eighteenth stage of
the Tour de France,
1986. The apparent
friendliness belies a
deep rivalry

Hinault after winning
his first Tour de France
in 1978

He was known as 'The Badger'. Some said it was the white headband against dark hair. But badgers are bastards, savage and tenacious. They don't give up – they just don't. Not a coincidence. Bernard Hinault looked mean when he rode, mean when he smiled, mean when he won. And there were plenty of wins: five Tours de France, three Giros d'Italia, two Vueltas à España, most of everything else. The dominant cyclist of the late 1970s and early '80s, and even better, he was French (as of 2015, no compatriot has won Le Tour, a source of national shame comparable to the Vichy regime).

Hinault's contribution to the technological history of the sport is significant – he worked with Look to develop the clipless pedal and took them to the peloton in 1984, whereupon they (slowly) overtook toe-clips. And Hinault's later story is that of two riders. The other: rival Greg LeMond, the Luke Skywalker to his Darth Vader, battling with lightweights instead of lightsabers; the blue-eyed, optimistic American against the elder, ruthless Frenchman. The fact they were teammates was irrelevant to their rivalry, which burned hot for a couple of years in the mid-'80s. Their side-by-side ascent of the Alpe d'Huez in the 1986 Tour was one of cycling's greatest duels, a passive-aggressive assertion of dominance against the backdrop of Hinault's apparent reneger on a promise to let LeMond win. LeMond came first anyway, The Badger was culled, and retired from the sport, but his legend lives on. As does he, on a farm in Brittany.

Luis Herrera

1961-

"Bernard Hinault told me that he wanted the stage.
I told him no, that we'd have to race for it. He was angry."
Luis Herrera

Luis Herrera ascends
between Pau and
Guzet-Neige in the
1984 Tour de France

Just as football has its centres of spiritual resonance – the seething arenas of South America, the muddy fields of England – so does cycling. It has a Western bias, and even then a tight focus, with a sweep across Continental Europe. But there's a global anomaly, 8,500km away from the dark cobblestones of Flanders: Colombia.

Since the 1950s this equatorial country has been sending riders to Europe to compete (and sending riders up peaks higher than anything France has to offer in the Vuelta à Colombia, first raced in 1951). In the 1980s they contributed to the internationalisation of the sport along with Brits, Americans and Aussies. In 1957 Fausto Coppi visited to take part in several so-called exhibition races with the Swiss

champion Hugo Koblet. Both found the Andes a lot harder to deal with than the Alps. Cycling was the national sport, and despite the ubiquity of football, it still is. Colombia has produced such luminaries as Ephraín Forero Triviño, winner of the first Vuelta à Colombia, the Olympic rider Ramón Hoyos and Roberto Escobar, whose exploits on a bicycle were somewhat overshadowed by the activities of his infamous brother Pablo.

But the rider who personifies most the Colombian spirit of cycling is Luis 'Lucho' Herrera, 'El Jardinerito', the Little Gardener, an unassuming, working-class man who did very special things on a bike. He was a climber in the classical sense, an elfin slip whose minimalist frame seemed like it

could never produce the power to send him up mountains. But it did: Lucho came first in a stage to L'Alpe d'Huez in 1984's Tour while still an amateur; he went on to win the Vuelta à España in 1987 and wore the King of the Mountains jerseys in all three grand tours. The Alpine ascents of the Critérium du Dauphiné Libéré proved happy hunting ground too: Lucho won in 1998 and 1991.

One of the secrets behind this country's success in cycling is altitude. Training at height increases the haematocrit level, leading to better endurance. And despite a few years where Colombia's lightweight hill-specialists lost out to the power-merchants of the '90s, they're back, notably in the form of ruthless Nairo Quintana, winner of the 2014 Giro d'Italia.

Laurent Fignon

1960-2010

"Within every champion there is a streak of spite,
brutality, violence, the urge to dominate… But in
cycling everyone, great and small, endures frequent
torture, physical and psychological. Sometimes
it's practically unfair."
Laurent Fignon

Laurent Fignon in a
time trial in the 1984
Tour de France

Above
Fignon leads a grim-looking pack on his way to winning the twentieth stage of the Tour de France, 1984

Opposite
Fignon, complete with trademark spectacles and headband, wears the pink jersey on the podium after the twentieth stage of the Giro d'Italia in 1984

Laurent Fignon did what no other pro cyclist did before or probably ever will again. He wore a sweatband a ponytail and little spectacles, and he did it with panache. The eyewear gained him the nickname 'Le Prof'.

The man from Montmartre had an amazing record: two Tour de France wins, one Giro d'Italia, classics including Milan-San Remo in 1989. But as well as that, he's remembered for one of the harshest losses in sporting history, up there with Maradona's hand of god. It seems cruel even to recount: in his flamboyantly brilliant autobiography he gets it out the way in the first chapter. So let's make it quick. Tour de France, 1989. After an open 20 stages, Fignon had 50 seconds over the next-placed Greg LeMond. The 24.5km time trial was practically a formality.

Except, a saddle-sore Fignon hadn't slept, and a confident LeMond was using a new (and, Fignon claimed, rule-bending) triathlon handlebar set-up. The Frenchman lost the Tour de France by eight seconds. "I simply couldn't get rid of the pain that was eating me up," he wrote afterwards. But try to forget about that nightmare – although he never did – and keep in mind a man who rode on the cusp of cycling eras old and new. Fignon admitted to amphetamine use but was disgusted by the thought of its newer, more biological, more effective relatives: hormone treatments, EPO. He retired in 1993, unwilling to ride in a peloton that accepted doping, unable to even physically compete. "It was as if I was already elsewhere," he said. The last rider of a golden age.

Greg LeMond

1961-

> "I don't remember a lot of racers' names, because
> I didn't race against people – I raced against myself."
> Greg LeMond

Greg Lemond takes
first, Sean Kelly takes
third at the 1989 World
Championships in
Chambéry, France

Forget that French-sounding surname – Greg LeMond is apple pie through and through, there's nothing *tart aux pommes* about him. When he began his invasion of Continental professional cycling in the early 1980s, he had the gee-whiz smile, the blond hair, the quarterback build. Moving from Nevada to join the Renault-Elf-Gitane team aged 21, LeMond was the American cat among the French pigeons: big and bold, unschooled in the local manners, unselfconsciously confident in his ability. And what an ability it was: LeMond was one of the most naturally gifted men to ever step on to a bike. His VO2 max (the efficiency with which the lungs supply oxygen to the blood) was perhaps the highest ever recorded in a cyclist. He rode without the crushing aggression of the likes of Merckx, but no one could stop him nonetheless. He was an instant success in Europe, winning a silver at the 1982 World Championships in England. He was the first (and now the only) American to win the Tour de France, in 1986, and won it another two times, in 1989 and 1990. The reason for the gap: he was shot in a hunting accident in 1987 and came within twenty minutes of bleeding to death.

His ascendance set him against Bernard Hinault, who by 1985 had won his fifth Tour de France and didn't want to stop; no one dared try to make him. Except LeMond, the young buck with no respect for reputation. Their rivalry was intense and real.

LeMond was a trailblazer, becoming a pro in Europe when most of his fellow countrymen had never heard of the Tour de France. But Americans love a champion and he was just that: there were more than a few stars and stripes among the crowds on the Champs-Elysée for his 1989 win. In 1985 the first American pro team, 7-11, entered the grand European tours, and the trickle of riders turned into a flow.

LeMond was one of those 'end of an era' riders, his era being pre-EPO. He abandoned the 1991 Tour de France due to not being able to keep up (although he cited mitochondrial myopathy too, a result of that hunting accident) and retired. He remains a larger-than-life force in US cycling; plus, unlike so many of the riders who have stood on the podium, LeMond seems like he'd be a great guy to have a beer with.

Above
Lemond in the twelfth
stage of the Tour de
France in 1986 – he
became the first
American to win the GC

Opposite
At the 1986 Tour de
France between Pau
and Superbagnéres,
Lemond draws ahead
of Bernard Hinault
(right) and Robert
Millar (left) on his way
to winning the stage

Lemond meets the
American film director
Michael Cimino (left)
and the actor Dustin
Hoffman. There were
reportedly discussions
around making a movie
about cycling, but it
was never realised

Miguel Indurain

1964-

"I am proud of what I have done, but you must keep a perspective. It's just a bicycle race, after all."
Miguel Indurain

Miguel Indurain
is a picture of
physiological
perfection in the
yellow jersey of the
Tour de France

You can't fight physiology. Legs, arms, core, heart and lungs – these are as much a part of the racing cyclist's arsenal as derailleur, cranks and frame. And when Miguel Indurain stepped over a top tube, the professional sport got itself a racing cyclist with a more impressive physiology than most. The man from Navarra in Spain was *the* tour specialist, winning five Tours de France in a row from 1990 onwards, usually with a high-five-style pair of Oakley shades on; two of those years, '92 and '93, he won the Giro d'Italia too, and in '94 he broke the Hour Record. (The succession of consecutive French victories has become a record since those of that Texan guy have been deleted from history.) And he won with something rare in the sport – sustained,

controlled domination. No crazed attacks, no snarling aggression, no ego or opportunism or breathtaking audacity. Indurain drew ahead on the flats, he held his own in the mountains and he just could not be caught in the time trials (which were often seriously longer in that era).

Fundamentally speaking, there's no requirement for a sportsman to be anything other than brilliant at his sport, and by all accounts Big Mig was just fine with that arrangement. Most describe him as an all-round lovely bloke, a bit shy, very calm, respectful, straightforward, moderate, discreet, modest: not the sort of qualities that turn an athletic star into a global superstar. But what Indurain may have lacked in gregarious personality, he made

up for with his body. His physiology has fascinated observers both scientific and sporting since his peak in the early '90s, and it has been analysed in forensically corporeal detail. He's 6' 1" and at his peak weighed around 78kg, which would traditionally make him too big to effectively challenge in the mountains. But he also had a frankly sloth-like resting heart rate of around 32; his muscles have a far greater number of 'slow twitch' fibres than 'quick' ones, making them less prone to the effects of lactic acid; his lung capacity was seven litres (double most people's); he has an almost perfect aerobic potential (or VO2 max, the efficiency of the lungs in working with oxygen); he had a powerful immune system and a supercharged metabolism.

Indurain at the men's time trial in the 1996 Atlanta Olympics. He was ideally suited to that discipline: he had power, stamina and control

Opposite
Indurain leads a climb in the 1994 Tour de France. He went on to win overall for a fourth consecutive time

There's no substitute for training, of course, but when blessed with these sort of metrics, the advantage is natural. Indurain was called a cyberman, an extraterrestrial, a superhuman. As sports science began to develop a greater understanding of biomechanics, of aerodynamics, of technology, powerful men and women like Indurain were granted an edge over the mercurial artists that had coloured road cycling for decades: the indefinable was now definable.

Given, however, that Indurain dominated the professional sport in the early 1990s when it's generally accepted that doping was rife, questions have begun to be asked. For his 2013 book *21 Counts*, former Festina coach and data obsessive Antoine Vayer

mapped the retrospective power outputs of twenty-one riders on a hill climb to produce a statistical model of relative performance. He groups the riders into categories from 'human' (clean) through 'miraculous' (dodgy) to 'mutant' (scarcely believable). If Vayer is to be believed, Indurain comes out top with an average power output of 455 watts. He characterises the early to mid-'90s as an EPO free-for-all, a time when the lack of an effective test meant that riders were free to dope to levels that would be impossible now. 'Bigger' cyclists, who may have traditionally won their points on the flats and the time trials, were now climbing like Colombians too. "I never failed a doping test" becomes a meaningless statement. The only major winner to emerge spotless

from this era, by Vayer's calculations, is Greg LeMond. In 2013 he famously cast doubt on Tour de France winner Chris Froome's data, to the great disdain of many who wanted to believe it was a clean win.

This all makes for fascinating reading for the sports fan and represents something potentially scandalous too, but not everyone is impressed by Vayer's video-based analysis. And none of this is meant to detract from Indurain's undoubtedly brilliant successes, it's only to highlight the debate that rages on in the sport. Whatever you choose to believe about Indurain, his wins are peerless, he never tested positive, he remains an all-round lovely bloke. You can't fight physiology and Indurain's was better than everyone's.

Graeme Obree

1965-

"Graeme Obree is unique: an artist of the pedal,
able to make his brain, his heart and his legs function
with the same effectiveness. A strange animal,
a very rare thoroughbred, and for this reason very
delicate just like a crystal."
Francesco Moser

Graeme Obree at the
Herne Hill Velodrome,
1993, before breaking
the outdoor Hour
Record. He also held
the men's ten-mile
TT record racing for
Leo RC

While the Scottish rider Graeme Obree's most notable moments came not on the road but on the track, he competed on the road too, but he's not only one of the most interesting people to have ever set out on a bicycle, he's one of the most interesting people full stop. How many other cyclists can say they've had a Hollywood film made about them? Lance Armstrong, of course, but he's probably not shouting about it.

Obree grew up in the west of Scotland, and by all accounts endured a miserable childhood. Like many kids, he escaped on his bike, and it was clear he had talent. An early aptitude for time trials shone through – an obsession with timing is a constant in his career, as is an unshakeable individuality – and that was coupled with an ability in road

races too. He became Scottish champion at junior and senior age groups, and won time trials at a Britain-wide level.

But despite a love for leaving it all behind on super-long tours, it was in the velodrome Obree's real obsession lay – in particular the ultimate solo prize, the Hour Record. In the late 1980s, when he set about it, it was Francesco Moser's 1984 time that was the one to beat. This was an age of technological confusion, with the UCI changing guidelines of what constituted a legal machine, sometimes retrospectively.

Every great cyclist needs a great rival, and Obree's was Chris Boardman. They couldn't have been more different – Boardman was bankrolled and professional, Obree was stoically self-funded (often

meagrely). Boardman went on to Tour de France and Olympic gold glory, Obree always stayed on the sidelines. But they both had the same fanatical attention to detail and the same belief that with the right equipment, human achievements could be extended to incredible lengths. They went head-to-head throughout the era, with Boardman also taking on the Hour Record. There they both made their greatest impacts. Boardman rode the famous Lotus Type 108, a single-shell carbon superbike generously subsidised by the sports car manufacturer. Obree rode Old Faithful, a revolutionary but resolutely DIY bicycle he made himself. In 1993 he took his invention to Norway and took the record with an unconventional 'tucked' cycling position.

Without the razor-sharp tanlines and big contracts of the pro peloton, without the multimillion-dollar R&D of the global bike manufacturers, the passion of the amateur still flourishes. Obree's is a story of innovation, of determination, of the outsider beating the odds. Nothing like it has been seen since. "There are lots of world champions," he said. "Not many people set world records."

Almost every part of his machine was groundbreaking, but the components the mainstream media latched on to were the bearings, which were cannibalised from Obree's washing machine. Cue loads of 'spin cycle'-type jokes, which showed the disregard most in Britain had for the sport at that time. It failed to acknowledge the genius and perseverance it took for an amateur to make his own bike and beat such a venerable record. In the end both his and Boardman's efforts were deemed illegal by the UCI and consigned to a fascinating chapter in cycling history.

Obree had a healthy disrespect for authority, which compounded his individualism. Depression meant his victories were tempered by existential emptiness; the lows in life were extra-deep. He attempted suicide more than once. He was offered a contract with a top French road team, but lasted a day – when he turned up and realised he was expected to dope, he walked away, he says, although in fairness he probably wasn't cut out for the regimented life of a pro.

Opposite
Obree settled in to his recognisable yet revolutionary tucked pose, which would later be outlawed by the UCI

Obree in the Yorkshire Dales. He has always attacked records as an amateur and outsider

Jeannie Longo

1958-

"She has been totally dominant for so long, and she has done it without any of the support or the money or the fame that the men get."
Graeme Obree

Jeannie Longo
celebrates winning the
women's criterium at
the 1983 Coors Classic
in Denver, Colorado

"Age and treachery will always overcome youth and skill," runs a quote sometimes attributed to the great Fausto Coppi. He died at 40; make of that what you will. At fifty-seven years old, Jeannie Longo was still competing in French racing: in a sport where riders in their thirties are considered veterans, she's pure vintage. In 2008, aged forty-nine, she came fourth in the Olympic road race (her seventh tournament in a row). As she's reached and passed the age where most in her position would be eyeing up the commentator's chair (or a deckchair somewhere sunny) she's won national time trials, day races and World Championships. Her record is enough to place her in the ranks of most-decorated riders ever, regardless of gender.

The fact that the Haute-Savoyard's victories are dominated by Olympic wins, rather than the classics and tours men usually race in, speaks volumes about the way the women's sport is still perceived. But public perception has never been high on Longo's list of things to care about. Despite regular fallings-out with the French national team and controversial pronouncements on politics, she remains one of the country's favourite athletes, proving that bike comes before pretty much everything there.

The only stain on a flawless career came in 2012, when her husband and trainer Patrice Ciprelli was indicted on charges of purchasing EPO from China. "I eat organic food," she told the *New York Times*. "I'm allergic to chemicals." She denies doping.

Opposite
The Coors Classic was
the USA's preeminent
cycling event of the era
and one of the biggest
in the world. Here the
pack speeds downhill
in 1985: Longo won
overall that year,
Bernard Hinault took
the men's title

Above
At 28, an age many
professional athletes
would consider their
peak, Longo won the
1986 pursuit World
Championships in
Grenoble, France, for
the second time

Robert Millar

1958-

"Fuck off."
Robert Millar

In the comic-book-
cool colours of the
Peugeot-Z team,
Robert Millar attacks
King of the Mountains
Gert-Jan Theunisse
in the 1989 Tour
de France

Despite a slight build suited to climbing, Millar could hold his own in a bunch. He's pictured second from left with Stephen Roche, Sean Kelly, Moreno Argentin and others at the 1983 Road Race Championships in Switzerland

Like a sparrow hopping from foot to foot, the polka-dotted Scotsman spins his way to a Pyrenean summit, sometimes accompanied by a grimacing set of hangers-on, often on his own. His left-right-left-right rhythm is metronomic and mesmerising. He seems to make the inclines tilt to flat. The year was 1984, the peak was in a late stage of the Tour de France, but it could have been 1983, 1986, 1989; Spain, Italy, Switzerland. He's the best British climber the sport has seen, at home in the hills like a snow-capped chalet. His career records were unsurpassed – King of the Mountains in 1984's Tour de France, winning at the vertiginous Pau-Guzet-Neige, and again in 1987's Giro d'Italia. Grand tour top-three placings. In 1990, the Critéterium

du Dauphiné in southeast France, won by the famous Brian Robinson thirty years before. Millar was heading to an almost-certain and potentially famous win at 1985's Vuelta España, but a conspiracy among Spanish riders (even those on his team) on the second-last stage ensured their own Pedro Delgado made up a big deficit and won ahead of the wee man. A travesty.

Millar was going where no British man had ever been before. Most of those back home had no idea how significant this type of high-altitude achievement was. And he did it without bravado. Did he even want to be there, leading the peloton up those impossible mountains?

He was born in Glasgow and brought a Calvinist attitude to work, aka cycling. Keep

your head down, get on with it, take pride. Work is identity. He was one of the most idiosyncratic men to ever pull on a cycling jersey. Aloof, isolated, driven, sarcastic, cynical, focused, difficult, introverted.

Back in the UK most sports fans were glued to Dennis Taylor beating Steve Davis in the World Snooker Championship final or Kenny Dalglish winning football's First Division in his first season in charge at Liverpool. Millar was making waves in cycling that didn't travel back across the English Channel, but still Granada Television made a documentary about him called *The High Life*. Accompanied by a motorik soundtrack, the startlingly slight Millar trains on open roads and talks about the realities of pro cycling at the top. He describes a

maverick break that upset the yellow jersey, earning him a rebuke: "I'm impressed with Hinault but I'm not impressed with his personality. I do what I want to do."

And what makes him so intriguing to modern cycling fans is that when he retired, he *retired*. He's rarely seen or heard. One of the most enigmatic men in cycling stayed so. No 'Millar'-branded midrange commuter bikes, no TV commentary. But it's not fair to say he disappeared – he's remained a spiky presence in cycling with columns in British magazines (most recently *Rouleur*), putting everything in perspective when it gets out of focus, bringing the brutal yet brilliant honesty of someone who has not given one thought to others' opinions since he first set off in a pro race in 1980.

Millar was one of the most gifted climbers the sport has ever known. He takes Charly Mottet up a hill in the tenth stage of the 1989 Tour de France

Marco Pantani

1970-2004

"To win, it's not drugs I need – it's mountains."
Marco Pantani

Marco Pantani after
winning the Alpe
d'Huez stage of the
1997 Tour France,
setting a new record of
37 minutes 35 seconds
for the climb

"Nobody has managed to understand me," said Marco Pantani, "not even my family. I am alone." So how should we even begin? The simplistic way would be to point to his successes – the towering Tour de France-Giro d'Italia double in 1998, a record ascent of Alpe d'Huez, unsurpassed since. The more profound way would be to go by what millions of sports fans saw around the world every time he clipped into his bicycle in the 1990s: the irresistible climbing style, as if he was being drawn up the mountains by a force inaccessible to the rest of the racers, as if he'd stopped to swap legs halfway up.

Memorably, his battles through high-altitude stages with the likes of Armstrong, Indurain and Pavel Tonkov were characterised by shocking, sudden, *sadistic* attacks that left him crossing hilltops solo. In contrast to the heavy-set pedallers who dominated the sport in that era, he had the trappings of a classic climber, with a featherweight frame and a cadence so fast it was almost a blur. What marked him out perhaps from some of the other great ascenders of history – Federico Bahamontes is a prime example – is the equally rapid way Pantani made it down the other side of the mountains he'd just conquered. He'd tuck himself *behind* the saddle and just let go, in a daredevil, some might say reckless, way that seemed to barely mask an outright contempt for life.

But to understand Pantani involves a lot more than watching him race, and that's where we must join his family and the rest of the confounded masses. He was born in the northeastern Emilia-Romagna district of Italy and from an early age felt uncomfortable in his own skin unless on a bicycle. His climbing prowess became apparent early on, but the awkwardness that built up in the face of everyday life never went away. It was managed with a self-enforced distance from those around him that was inevitably taken for arrogance. He was different: outspoken, enigmatic, cryptic, mercurial. A diamond stud nose ring and, later, hoop earring and bandana meant he stood out from the increasingly uniform peloton.

He became a superstar in his native Italy, perhaps the brightest since Coppi. In sport Italian fans love a flawed genius above all,

Opposite

Pantani ascended with
frightening power. He's
pictured here in the
1998 Tour de France,
in which he won the
overall GC

Below

Pantani in 1995,
another year in which
he won the famous
Alpe d'Huez stage of
the Tour de France

especially one who tears himself inside out, dashes his heart against the road in the name of sporting spectacle – but Pantani was to the end a troubled soul.

That end came too soon. Halfway through 1999's Giro d'Italia a blood test showed a haematocrit percentage higher than 50, which was the almost arbitrary figure the UCI had proclaimed to be the 'healthy' level for a cyclist free from the side-effects of EPO. Cycling was Pantani's life – his "language", as he put it – so when cycling went wrong, life went wrong. The twin pressures of celebrity and existential disquiet drove Pantani to excess both on the bike and off it, which meant life-changing volumes of cocaine. His racing career, for the first time, was all downhill; he was overcome by depression and solitude and died paranoid, broken and alone in a resort hotel room in Rimini from the effects of a drug overdose. It was Valentine's Day, he was aged 34. Since then fanatical supporters have made wild claims about his demise, claiming Mafia involvement, set-ups and cover-ups.

Willy Voet, the Festina soigneur behind the Festina scandal of 1998, once said, "Just as money doesn't create happiness but goes a long way towards it, doping doesn't create a champion but doesn't do him any harm either." Regarding the EPO accusations Pantani claimed innocence and cried conspiracy. However he won, though, he did it with sophistication, and there's no shortcut to that.

Wim Vansevenant
1971-

"If someone hears my name they say, ah! It's the lanterne rouge of the Tour de France. I think it's the most important thing in my whole cycling career."
Wim Vansevenant

Wim Vansevenant in a time trial stage of the 2006 Tour de France, a year in which he finished heroically last

Jacques Pfister and Perre Claes, second-last and last-placed in the 1927 Tour de France, with the symbolic *lanterne rouge*

Arsène Millocheau did it before anyone else. Tony Hoar did it for the British on his debut. But only one man did it three times in a row: finishing last in the Tour de France and gaining the title of 'lanterne rouge', the red lantern, after the light that used to swing from the end carriage on a train. The opposite of the yellow jersey, and a whole lot less practical to wear.

The Belgian Wim Vansevenant is the holder of this record, which to the uninitiated seems ignominious but in its own way is as impressive as winning. That Nike attitude – 'second place is the first loser' – is impractical and unrealistic. In recent years of the Tour de France, around 20 percent of the almost-200 at the starting line haven't even made it to

the end, be it down to illness, collision, catastrophic failure of machine or body, or simply dissolution of will. If anyone who ever makes it far enough in their career to even contemplate riding the toughest endurance race on earth could be called a loser, it would be those who aborted, those who get 'DNF' (did not finish) unceremoniously suffixed to their name. But to simply make it to the end is to share in the glory of the event, and the lower-placed riders often have a more interesting story to tell. One-hundred-and-sixty-fourth place is the hundred-and-sixty-fourth winner.

Wim Vansevenant brought up the rear to the very end of Le Tour thrice in the mid-2000s. But the ultimate placing was little to do with failure and everything to do with

sacrifice and pragmatism. The writer Max Leonard loved the romance of the lanterne rouge so much he made a whole book about it, and described meeting Wim on his Flanders farm to hear about the prosaic realities of cycling life far from the podium. "Normal life sucks," Wim told him. "When you are a cyclist you don't have to think, you just pedal."

Wim was a *domestique*, one of those everyman riders whose job is to work for the team captain – venture first up the lower slopes, shield the main man from the headwinds and sidewinds, initiate breakaways, offer advice on the course of the route, donate water bottles or wheels or whole bikes if necessary, then drop back into anonymity when the proper kick to the

finish begins. A cross between a caddy, a valet and a wingman. The *domestique de luxe*, an exclusive subcategory, might have the thighs to win a sprint or the lungs for a big climb, but mostly their names appear inconsequentially down the rankings. In Wim's case, he accepted he wasn't good enough to reach the pinnacle of the sport, but for pride, sense of servitude and plain old cash, he cycled his arse off for his friend Peter van Petegem and the Lotto-Domo team in races all over Europe. Last-place finishes not only brought a bit of lighthearted attention, they ensured no unnecessary energy was expended. And for those of us who dream of racing, it has to be accepted that being the best *domestique* is still being the best.

Vansevenant completes the second stage of the 2007 Tour de France, a year in which he finished… last

Andrei Kivilev

1973-2003

"Kivilev was very unlucky not being able to react,
it is fate, he was very unlucky. But please stop the
discussion about the helmet."
Laurent Fignon

Andrei Kivilev in the
eleventh stage of the
2003 Tour de France

Sportsmen and women often think about their legacy. How will they be remembered? By the time the very best leave their chosen discipline, things aren't the same: they've moved the goalposts, set the bar higher, changed the game. Look at the dates up there underneath Andrei Kivilev's name: 1973-2003. Twenty-nine years old. In the second stage of the 2003 Paris-Nice race, the Kazakh fell heavily after rider contact and didn't get back up. He went into a coma in hospital and died the next day from head injuries caused by the impact. His career was in the ascendence: he'd won the Route du Sud in 2001 and came fourth in the Tour de France the same year.

A couple of weeks after Kivilev's death, the UCI indicated it would support the compulsory wearing of helmets in pro races. Unlike previous attempts to introduce such measures, peloton protest was muted. To this day, not everyone is convinced of their efficacy, just as Laurent Fignon wasn't in 2003, but now the idea of not wearing helmets is unthinkable, like smoking on aeroplanes. Kivilev's legacy is unignorable, but it's not one anyone would have wanted.

Floyd Landis

1975-

"I ended up making a living in a sport where the men wear spandex and shave their legs – and that's not even the funny part. The funny part is that cycling and its anti-doping program are run by people so incompetent they couldn't even run a Ralph's grocery store."

Floyd Landis, in his 2007 autobiography
Positively False

Floyd Landis climbs
Taylor Street in the San
Francisco Grand Prix
in 2001

Landis, in the yellow jersey, climbs in the sixteenth stage of the 2006 Tour de France

It would be nice if this book had no mention of drugs, performance-enhancing or otherwise. But this isn't a book about Ultimate Frisbee, it's about road cycling. For decades, the issue wasn't so much an elephant in the room, more a whole herd of them balancing on balls like Victorian circus performers. The sport is difficult, and most riders realised from the start: anything that could make it easier to *finish* – let alone easier to win – was to be gratefully accepted. It was kill or be killed, dope or be dropped

In his quote on the previous page, Floyd Landis may have a point about the authorities, although his admission in 2010 that he was doping all along has turned his autobiography into a monumental work of irony. In Landis's day UCI testing

would identify the odd 'bad apple', who would usually be back on their bike in a few months. The beginning of this new era of recognition was 8th July 2008, when a car driven without licence by Belgian soigneur Willy Voet of the Festina team was stopped at the French border en route to the *Grand Départ* in Dublin. It was found to be carrying a whole pharmacy's worth of various illegal products, all of the performance-enhancing variety, including erythropoietin (EPO, described as "the perfect drug" by Lance Armstrong). It came to public attention, along with the fact that there was a big secret in cycling – many professional road cyclists were cheating, although everyone involved preferred the oleaginously euphemistic 'being prepared'. It led to raids, arrests, then bans, abandonments, shame, outrage and a deep distrust that the sport still wears heavy almost two decades later.

"Amphetamines injected into the arms or the stomach, corticoids, steroids, anabolic agents, even testosterone injected into the buttock muscles. Daily rituals, nothing out of the ordinary," Voet wrote in his exposé *Breaking the Chain*. Campaigning journalists like David Walsh and Paul Kimmage (a former pro) were persecuted for speaking out against doping, by the very people who knew the scale of its existence.

After stage 17 of 2006's Tour de France, Floyd Landis gave a urine sample which testing showed contained a high level of synthetic testosterone. He won the General Classification days later, only to be disqualified almost instantly. It was the year after his US Postal Service teammate Lance Armstrong had won his seventh consecutive GC: Landis should have represented a new age of American cycling. The pair's relationship, however, turned caustic after Landis's expulsion and stigmatisation; his exposure of the whole culture of doping eventually led to Armstrong's downfall. They ended up in court and stayed there – in 2016, a $100m 'whistleblower' case Landis filed against Armstrong on behalf of the US government is ongoing. The Postal Service wants its sponsorship money back; if the suit is successful Landis could get a third. That would be a win, but not the sort he imagined when he set out as a wide-eyed young pro in '99.

Below

Landis forms part of a breakway between Agde and Ax-Trois-Domaines in the 2005 Tour de France along with others including Ivan Basso, Jan Ullrich and his compatriot Lance Armstrong (in the yellow jersey)

Next page

The sort of sweeping view the Tour de France has become famous for – race leader Chris Froome in a group passing between Saint-Jean-de-Maurienne and La Toussuire in the Alps, 2015

Lance Armstrong

1971-

"For me, living life to the fullest is a lot about testing myself: accepting challenges, training hard, and then going for it. No way I'm spending the rest of my days avoiding goals. As far as I'm concerned, *that* would wreck my legacy."

Lance Armstrong, in his autobiography *My Comeback*

For seven years between 1999 and 2005, Lance Armstrong was hardly out of the Tour de France yellow jersey, as he was here in 2004

Above
Armstrong the athlete
of devastating power
and stamina

Opposite
Reinforcing what had
become an annual
event in France,
Armstrong celebrates
another stage win in
the 2004 Tour

Armstrong the global
sporting superstar
faces the cameras

It could have been about the boy who wanted only to beat everyone else, since his triathlon days as a teenager in Texas. It could have been about the young man who stuck with bicycle racing in the US when its popularity as a spectator sport was somewhere below rodeo and wrestling, and who inspired a generation with his Livestrong foundation. The fairytale comeback after cancer, the millions of pounds raised for charity. It could have been about a record seven Tour de France victories, or the elevation to the global celebrity sportsman podium beside Tiger Woods, Michael Jordan, OJ Simpson. It could have been about that legendary feint-then-attack on the final climb of the Alpe d'Huez in 2001. But it's not. The

Lance legacy isn't winning, it's doping. If this book only profiled honest riders, it would be a slim volume: he's in illustrious company when it comes to outlawed chemical performance-enhancements. The pharmaceutical history of this sport is shamefully rich, but Armstrong's era was a spike on the charts.

And as everyone knows, it wasn't just the drugs that finished him, it was his deception, his destruction, his deceit. Rivals on and off the road encountered the same ruthlessness, and in the end what made Armstrong so successful brought him down. But the passage of time insists we put him in context. The Festina affair of 1998, in which the realities of doping were laid bare to a large viewing audience for the

first time, cast an uncomfortably probing spotlight on the riders of Armstrong's day. So what about the ones that came before? Some of the big winners of the early '90s achieved quite literally incredible feats. And does anyone really dope to win, knowing that the victory will forever be hollow? Or did he do it just to keep up, just to maintain the superman image (and the supersized contracts)?

He wasn't the only one, he just fell the hardest. Armstrong's isn't the last page in the EPO saga, but it might be near the end of the chapter. Remember the disgrace, but don't forget that superpowered climber, the turbocharged time trialist with the set-jawed steel and all-encompassing focus on the finish line.

Sarah Storey

1977-

"I started out in life not even realising the Paralympic Games existed… For me it's just sport."
Sarah Storey, quoted in *The Guardian*

Sarah Storey on her way to becoming Britain's most decorated Paralympian, winning gold in the women's individual C4-5 road race in the London 2012 Paralympic Games

Bicycling is freedom, but sometimes freedom is hard-fought. It should be the easiest thing in the world to hop on a bike and set off, but as the likes of Major Taylor and Frances Willard have shown, marginalisation is an obstacle to riding greater than any pothole. Cycling was first introduced to the Paralympics in 1984 and grew to include visually impaired tandem track events as well as tricycling, handcycling and races using adapted bicycles not unlike machines for able-bodied riders. It's in this environment that Sarah Storey, who was born with a partially formed left hand, became Britain's most decorated Paralympian, winning gold medals in time trials at Beijing 2008 and London 2012 on both road and track

(including a quite incredible four in 2012: time trial, pursuit, road race and 500m time trial). This is all on top of a previous, lavishly garlanded career as a Paralympic swimmer, which began as far back as Barcelona 1992.

Many – most – histories of cycling completely ignore the experience of less able-bodied riders, amateur or athletic. But the growing interest in cycling as a whole leads to the fact that it doesn't take much to adapt a bike for a range of users – it is, after all, one of the most evolved inventions in human history. And although Sarah Storey is eligible to enter parasport events, she's competed and won in many pro road race events with her own team, Podium Ambition.

David Millar

1977-

"Cycling is mad, beautifully so. The beauty, suffering, grandeur and panache are what make it special."
David Millar

David Millar forms a sleek aerodynamic shape in the elite men's time trial at the 2006 World Championships in Salzburg, Austria

Millar wears the pink
leader's jersey on
the gravel roads of
Tuscany in the fifth
stage of the Giro
d'Italia, 2011

Opposite
Millar won several
grand tour stages in
his career: here he
celebrates crossing
the line first in the
twelfth stage of the
2012 Tour de France

At the 2011 Tour
de France, Millar
(here with Christian
Vandevelde) finished
well in several stages,
and his team Garmin-
Cervelo won the GC

As well as having the distinction of being the first Brit to have worn the leader's jersey in all three European grand tours, this undeniably suave Scot has the distinction of being one of those cyclists to look as good off the bike as on it. Cycling has had its fair share of dandies: maybe it's the sport's inherent Frenchness, maybe it's the lithe and inevitably tanned bodies, maybe it's the unavoidable rakishness of an insouciantly placed *casquette*. Look at the way Coppi wore his grace like an expensive suit, or at De Vlaeminck in his Brooklyn top before the word 'hipster' had even been co-opted.

However, before we allow Millar's flair to overshadow his achievements, let's remember the British road and TT wins in 2007, and the fact he still is the only British rider to have worn the yellow, green, white and polka-dot jerseys in the Tour de France, on top of podium finishes in Commonwealth Games and World Championships.

He left behind the safety and security of his homeland early in life to take the only route open to those in his position: he dived headfirst into professional cycling, joining a French team and learning the ropes in the toughest way possible, back in the days when the sport in Britain was underfunded, underresourced and underloved. Millar has been scathingly open about the use of drugs in cycling, both performance-enhancing and otherwise, and he's brutally honest about the way he resisted but then succumbed to the overwhelming force of the mid-2000s peloton. His tale of the descent of a naive, talented young lad into a cynical, desperate pro is heartbreaking and horrifying. Observers often talk of EPO as a whispered secret, everywhere but nowhere. The confidence and closed ranks is yet another thing that allowed professional cyclists to imagine they are different from the rest of the human world.

Millar was banned in 2004 for two years after admitting to using EPO, but since his comeback refused to be another of those 'shrug, ah well, business as usual' convicts. He's been one of the loudest voices calling for a clean-up. Those disappointed at his retiral in 2014 may be cheered by the fact that he now has a line of clothing, Chpt III, through which amateurs may attempt to absorb some of that suavity. Worth a try.

Bradley Wiggins

1980-

"It goes uphill like all the others, doesn't it?"
Bradley Wiggins on the 2,100m Pyrenean
Col du Tourmalet

Bradley Wiggins on
his way to winning
the Elite Men's British
National Time Trial
Championships in
2014 in Wales. He has
the staying power
and ability to lock into
a perfect position
that makes him a
formidable time trialler

Wiggins: the British Armstrong. Not like that. Cycling lags far behind football, rugby and other less 'Continental' sports in terms of popularity – how could the British *truly* love a discipline that measures distance in kilometres – but no cycling sportsman captured the public imagination there more effectively than Wiggo. His acceleration from just another guy on a bike to velodrome star to national hero hit a peak over summer 2012 – in July he became the first British man to win the Tour de France, then at the Olympics (conveniently in London) he beat them all in the time trial. Those early achievements by British professional cyclists – Robinson, Simpson, Hoban, Millar – seemed quaint, almost. But it's not just the wins that won over a nation – it's

the Jam hairdo, the everyman geniality, the laconic witticisms, the occasional beard. ("Why shave your legs then grow a beard?" the ignorant might wonder. Look at him, that's why.) The big money of Team Sky helped too, no doubt. This outfit was set up in 2010 in a way that revolutionised cycling not just in Britain but across the sport. It was luxuriously funded, but at its core is a dedication not just to winning but nurturing young national talent and even altruistic ideas; three British Tour de France wins in four years captivated the country and has led to huge increases in bicycle use. All the others have to try a bit harder now.

Everyone loves Wiggins because he's not a machine, he's a man – 'Le Gentleman', as the French dubbed him. If a British cyclist

can win over the French, you know he's got something special. Did being born in Flanders to a pro track cyclist father help too? He grew up in Kilburn, northwest London. It was from these beginnings that this most versatile of riders began an ascent to the top, which took in Olympic track golds, Commonwealth medals, grand tour and classic wins, and then in 2015, the Hour Record, broken at Lee Valley Velopark. This simple but impossibly difficult feat of precision riding and all-out endurance has long attracted the top road racers – in this book alone, Miguel Indurain, Eddy Merckx and Francesco Moser among others all took the title. The first holder was one Henri Desgrange, founder of the Tour de France. Oh, and Bradley is now Sir Bradley, to you.

Opposite
In the 2012 Tour de France, Wiggins leads his Sky teammate Chris Froome in the eleventh stage. Wiggins and Froome came first and second in the GC

Below
Wiggins in the 2014 Paris-Roubaix, on a Pinarello machine specially modified to alleviate the stresses of riding the *pavés*

Wiggins in the yellow jersey with another British teammate, Mark Cavendish

Nicole Cooke

1983-

"Since the age of 12, I had dreamed of winning the Tour de France. On the TV, I had watched Robert Millar climbing the mountains. I had ridden the French Alps on our family camping holidays, dreaming as I was climbing that I was on my own ahead of the pack, heading to victory. Now I was standing on the start line wearing the yellow jersey, about to begin a stage that was going to take us over the famous Mont Ventoux, a climb of special magic to all British riders."

Nicole Cooke, in *The Breakaway: My Story*

Nicole Cooke at the
Women's Elite Time
Trial at the 2006
UCI Road World
Championships
in Salzburg, Austria

Cooke takes gold at the women's road race at the 2008 Beijing Olympic Games

Opposite
Another event, another win: the Elite women's road race at the 2008 UCI Road World Championships in Varese, Italy

Imagine being in a race and you're in front because you're the best and no one else can catch you. Your success is so nailed-on the bookies have already paid out. But then people keep placing obstacles in your way. A cartoon scatter of tacks, fallen trees. It's going to take a lot more than cycling skills to get where you want to be. This theatrical vision is a metaphor for the career of Nicole Cooke. The massively talented champion from Wales came up against barriers to success from the start, almost all of them excuses from others as to why she shouldn't be a pro: her bike wasn't good enough, she was too young, she won with luck, she lived in the wrong country, and, most frequently of all, she was female. There are many women represented in this book, and most

share the same experience: whether it's upon a penny farthing or a top-level carbon machine, there seems to be someone there telling them they can't do it.

Fortunately, Cooke either ignored, laughed at or kicked back against obfuscation and prejudice and went on to win like no one else. That she was one of Britain's best cyclists is without question; she was the first Brit to win the Tour de France (2006 and 2007, sorry Wiggo) and added one Giro d'Italia GC to her palmarès along with a Commonwealth Games road race gold (2002), an Olympic road gold and a World Championship, as well as just about all the classics open to her.

There's a lot of talk about the 'omerta' in cycling: the code of silence that keeps dirty

secrets secret for so long. If it were a real mafia-enforced edict, Cooke would be in hiding. Her life on a bike is one of success matched by excoriating takedowns of everyone who stood in her way. The UCI, British Cycling, the Welsh Cycling Union, the IOC, professional teams, sponsors, coaches and unsporting rivals, plus assorted bean-counters, foot-draggers, pen-pushers and plain old sexists all come under righteous attack. This isn't to say she was difficult – in the pantheon of professional riders, in which some come across as positively sociopathic, she's just an ordinary Welsh lass who happens to be brilliant at cycling. It is to say that Cooke beat everything and everyone in her way, and that's maybe harder than just winning races.

Chris Froome

1985-

"I like to suffer. I like it better when I know that the people around me are suffering too."
Chris Froome

Exertions over, Froome toasts a Tour win in the traditional way on the Champs-Elysée, 2015

The French uncharacteristically took a British rider to their hearts in Bradley Wiggins, but it was business as usual when Chris Froome won the Tour de France in 2013 and 2015. The British have been reluctant to throw themselves behind Froome too, to be fair, and not because he was born and raised in Africa (Wiggins was born in Belgium, after all). He is, by all accounts, a lovely chap, but his skillset doesn't include media-friendly quips; he's sober rather than sardonic, matter-of-fact rather than off-the-cuff. "More machine than man," they might say: untrue, but cycling is a sport that loves heroic losers, tempestuous madmen, outspoken outsiders, monstrous egos – and when an ordinary guy pulls on a victor's jersey, it's just no fun.

Froome is one of the most well-regarded riders of recent years, well on his way to being 'the tour rider of his generation', but the beauty of his wins are matched by the cynicism of sports journalists. Everyone's interested in his numbers and some refuse to believe they add up. Post-Armstrong, this solidly brilliant rider's power output, VAM ('velocità ascensionale media', average climbing speed), cadence and heartrate has been pored over by analysts amateur and professional alike – they don't like that he came almost from nowhere to win and win big; they point to middling performances in previous events. A video of his victorious ascent of Mont Ventoux was uploaded to YouTube with accompanying second-by-second physiological data supposedly stolen from a hacked Team Sky computer. That's how seriously people take this.

"Chris, prouve-nous qu'on peut aussi croire en toi" ("Show us that we can believe in you too"), said a provocative *Le Monde* headline. Roadside critics have shown their displeasure in less subtle ways – a cup of piss in his direction during Stage 14 of 2015's Tour de France.

Froome is the most visibly successful yet inscrutable face of his team Sky's micro-scientific approach to bicycle racing, which insists upon "the best equipment, the best back-up staff, the best experts to research every area from diet to aerodynamics", as former teammate Wiggins puts it. (And with Wiggins, Froome provided one of the more interesting contemporary intrateam rivalries,

Opposite
A lake between Digne-les-Bains and Pra Loup makes a beautiful backdrop for the pack in the seventeenth stage of the Tour de France, 2015

Below
With the Arc de Triomphe behind, Froome takes the yellow jersey to the finish of the 2013 Tour

Next page
In 2015 Froome became the first British man to win two Tour de France GCs. Here he rides in the peloton during the stage that he took in Alpe d'Huez

those that are inevitable when two GC riders wear the same colours.)

'Marginal gains' is Sky's buzzphrase, and it amounts to total cycling: as far from the wine-and-speed-guzzling semi-amateurs of old as it's possible to get. The team is perceived by some as a corporate sports factory, but if you're riding clean, you need more than hard work to win, and marginal gains win races. Froome's story illustrates something else: the way science has edged out some of the romance of road cycling. We knew Merckx was great without seeing his power data. The more we analyse, the less is left to chance, the more predictable it becomes. Let's hope the radical spirit of cycling is strong enough to render the numbers just numbers.

Marianne Vos

1987-

"I would like to see a future where little girls can dream of that yellow jersey and not be told no."
Marianne Vos, quoted in *Bicycling*

Marianne Vos wins the
women's road race at
the very British 2012
Olympic Games

Opposite
**Marianne Vos in the
Dutch orange during
the UCI Elite women's
road race in 2013 in
Florence, Italy**

Above
**Marianne Vos
(left) beats Lizzie
Armitstead into
second place in the
women's road race
at the London 2012
Olympics**

There's no way this book could feature the careers of Merckx, Coppi, Hinault, Fignon, Wiggins, without including Marianne Vos. To do so would be to ignore the incredible achievements of one of the finest cycling athletes in history (and she's still young). Because of a well-publicised lack of publicity around women's cycling her story is less well-known than the top men in the sport, but like Merckx, she wins just about everything she enters. 'The female Eddy Merckx' is the comparison made most often, and there isn't really much higher praise a cyclist could get. Her style, like his, is based on supreme, all-conquering strength, physical and mental, so that to stop because of anything other than devastating illness or mechanical misadventure is not an option. ("I can't really get that people see me like him," she said in an interview. "Of course, I win some races, but I'm not so special.")

Her palmarès is way too extensive to do justice to here, but it's safe to say, if it involved bicycles and just about any form of competition, it's on it – road, track and cyclocross championships, an Olympic gold, stage races, one-days, classics, time trials. It runs into pages. Vos is now in the unusual position of being so dominant in her sport that secretly, race organisers probably wish she might not turn up so someone else could get a chance. It's no exaggeration to say that she's the best cyclist in the world. And what's more, she has years ahead of her. Look out, Eddy.

Peter Sloterdijk

1947-

"The relationship between sports and everyday life is like that between the holy and the mundane. It forms a model world, in which everything we know from the average world is intensified."
Peter Sloterdijk

Vicente Trueba climbs the Col du Tourmalet in the 1933 Tour de France. Since its inception, road cycling has presented opposing characteristics: suffering and health, work and freedom

Ottavio Bottecchia
in the 1923 Tour de
France. In a sport that
has had glorious status
bestowed upon it, he
represents toil, poverty
and mortality

Peter Sloterdijk is a cycling philosopher or a philosophising cyclist. Over his long career the German has straddled the worlds of academic and popular philosophy; in 2008 he gave a typically eloquent interview to the magazine *Der Spiegel* in which he described the horror he felt at the sport's dopers, compared with the awe of their prowess brought on by his own amateur ascent of the mighty Mont Ventoux. With his symbolic interpretations of cycling, he perpetuates a long tradition of writers turning their attentions to an essentially humble but contradictory pursuit. For the vast majority of those who ride bicycles, to do so is simply a convenient way to travel. It's not glorious, it's not lucrative, there's no suffering: it's actually quite pleasant. Those

who make their money from it are a tiny minority, yet are granted legendary status. What is it about road cycling that has attracted such grand-scale mythologising?

The French surrealist Alfred Jarry seems like he might agree: he was a fanatical and energetic cyclist, bemoaning those other riders who, "thinking themselves poets, slow down en route to contemplate the view". But he joins in with the lionising of cycling in his proto-sci-fi novel of 1902, *Supermale* – it involves a transcontinental jet-paced bike race in which riders fuelled by 'Perpetual Motion Food' transcend their human selves to achieve superhuman feats of athleticism.

The idea was taken up with new insight by the philosopher Roland Barthes, who in

a 1955 essay *The Tour de France as Epic* elevates the event beyond mere bike race and up into a rarefied space where man and nature not only battled but took on characteristics of each other. And he too recognises the role of the writer in creating the perfect myth: "Language's role is enormous here, it is language which gives the event – ineffable because ceaselessly devolved into duration – the epic promotion which allows it to be solidified."

The only other sport that's had a comparable level of serious intellectual attention is boxing, which shares with cycling suffering, danger as spectacle, and the necessity of absolute dedication. It's no surprise that Ernest Hemingway was a fan of European cycling. He loved its machismo and extremes, but avoided writing on it at length: just as the language of music is Italian, the language of cycling is French, and Hemingway thought his blunt American English could never do it justice.

"If you pull down the sport's dimension of honour, and its symbols, everything ends," said Sloterdijk. For him the myth is dead, killed by doping and the race towards physiological and technological perfection. But let's leave the last word to someone who really knows what he's talking about. "People ride a bike as a child and think they know what we go through," said Bernard Hinault. "They should all shut up." Maybe he has a point. Like many things, it's one thing to write about it, better to do. Wouldn't we all rather be on a bike?

Above
The 1949 Paris-Roubaix. The idea of cycling races as a thrilling spectacle has existed since the first bicycles were ridden

Next page
A cycling race without cyclists: spectators await the leaders in the French Alps during the 1926 Tour de France

Index

Index

Bibliography

Bicycle: The History, David V Herlihy

Breaking the Chain, Willy Voet

The Climb, Chris Froome

Coppi e Bartali, Curzio Malaparte

Coppi: Inside the Legend of the Campionissimo, Herbie Sykes

Cutting Edge Cycling: Advanced Training for Advanced Cyclists, Hunter Allen and Stephen S Cheung

Cycling, October 7 and 14 1893

Cycling is My Life, Tommy Simpson

Cycling: Philosophy for Everyone, ed Jesús Ilundáin-Agurrazza and Michael W Austin

The Cycling Physiology of Miguel Indurain 14 Years After Retirement, Iñigo Mujika, in the *International Journal of Sports Physiology and Performance*

The Death of Marco Pantani: a Biography, Mark Rendell

Eddy Merckx: The Cannibal, Daniel Friebe

La Fabuleuse Histoire du Tour de France, Pierre Chany and Thierry Cazeneuve

Fallen Angel: The Passion of Fausto Coppi, William Fotheringham

The Fastest Bicycle Rider in the World, Marshall W 'Major' Taylor

The Flying Scotsman, Graeme Obree

French Cycling: A Social and Cultural History, Hugh Dauncey

The Giro d'Italia: Coppi versus Bartali at the 1949 Tour of Italy, Dino Buzzati

Gli Anni Ruggenti di Alfonsina Strada, Paolo Facchinetti

To the Golden Gate: George Nellis' 1887 Wheel Across the Continent, Charles Meinert, on www.thewheelmen.org

Greg LeMond: The Incredible Comeback, Samuel Abt

Hearts of Lions: The History of American Cycling, Peter Nye

The History of Cycling in Fifty Bikes, Tom Ambrose

Hunger, Sean Kelly

This Island Race: Inside 135 Years of British Bike Racing, Les Woodland

In Search of Robert Millar, Richard Moore

Kelly, David Walsh

Kings of the Mountains, Matt Rendell

Kings of the Road, Robin Magowan

From Lance to Landis: Inside the Doping Controversy at the Tour de France, David Walsh

Lanterne Rouge: The Last Man in the Tour de France, Max Leonard

Le Tour: A History of the Tour de France, Geoffrey Wheatcroft

Louison Bobet: Une Vélobiographie, Jean Bobet

Maglia Rosa: Triumph and Tragedy at the Giro d'Italia, Herbie Sykes

Marguerite Wilson: The First Star of Women's Cycling, William Wilson

Miguel Indurain: A Life on Wheels, Pablo Muñoz

Mostly Middle-Class Cycling Heroes: The Fin-de-Siècle Commercial Obsession with Speed, Distance and Records, Andrew Ritchie and Rüdiger Rabenstein, in Reformers, Sport, Modernizers: Middle-class Revolutionaries, ed JA Mangan

The Monuments: The Grit and Glory of Cycling's Greatest One-Day Races, Peter Cossins

My Time, Bradley Wiggins

My Comeback: Up Close and Personal, Lance Armstrong

Mythologies, Roland Barthes

Not Normal?, Antoine Vayer

Pedalare! Pedalare! A History of Italian Cycling, John Foot

Personal Best, Beryl Burton

Quest for Speed: Early Bicycle Racing 1868-1903, Andrew Ritchie

The Race Against the Stasi: the Incredible Story of Dieter Wiedemann, the Iron Curtain and the Greatest Cycling Race on Earth, Herbie Sykes

A Race For Madmen: The Extraordinary History of the Tour de France, Chris Sidwells

The Racer, David Millar

Racing Through the Dark, David Millar

Road To Valour: Gino Bartali, Tour de France Legend and Italy's Secret World War Two Hero, Aili and Andres McConnon

Roule Britannia, Charles Fotheringham

Seven Deadly Sins: My Pursuit of Lance Armstrong, David Walsh

Sex, Lies and Handlebar Tape: The Remarkable Life of Jacques Antequil, Paul Howard

Slaying the Badger: LeMond, Hinault and the Greatest Ever Tour de France, Richard Moore

The Story of the Giro d'Italia: A Year-by-Year History of the Tour of Italy, Volume 1: 1909-1970, Bill McGann and Carol McGann

Taming the Bicycle, Mark Twain

Tessie Reynolds: A 'Rational' Activist, Morgan E Barlow, in *Proceedings of the 23rd International Cycling History Conference*

Tomorrow, We Ride, Jean Bobet

Tour de France: The Complete History of the World's Greatest Cycle Race, 10th Edition, Marguerite Lazell

We Were Young and Carefree, Laurent Fignon

Wheels of Chance, HG Wells

A Wheel Within a Wheel: How I Learned to Ride the Bicycle, Frances Willard

The World on Wheels, HO Duncan

You Must Change Your Life, Peter Sloterdijk

On Your Bicycle: an Illustrated History of Cycling, James McGurn

Picture credits

Akg-images: p81, p83; Interfoto / Friedrich
p49, p50

Alamy: Allan Cash Picture Library p91; Stephen
Fleming p143

Alembic Rare Books p23 left

Courtesy of Charles Meinert p29

The Dancing Chain by Frank Berto, courtesy
of Cycle Publishing p33

Courtesy of Dieter Wiedemann p97

Courtesy of Dumfries and Galloway Council
Libraries, Information and Archives p15, p16
bottom

Frances E Willard Memorial Library p21

Getty: p73, p93, p123; AFP front cover, p6-7,
p46 bottom, p67, p85, p95, p102 top, p105,
p106, p107, p122 top, p129, p130, p131, p197;
Bob Thomas/Popperfoto p39; Brian Brainerd
p118; Bride Lane Library p52-53; Bryn Lennon
p175, p179, p180, p181 bottom, p181 top,
p184, p185, p187, p189, p190-191, p194, p195,
back cover; Carl de Souza p183; David Madison
p121, p163; Duane Howell p117, p119, p147;
Eric Feferberg p188; Fotosearch p19; Franck
Fife p159, p164, p165, p170 bottom, p176 top;
Friedemann Vogel p171; Gabriel Duval p101;
Gerard Malie p146; Gilbert Uzan p122 bottom;
Haywood Magee p11; Hulton Archive p22, p23
right, p94; Javier Sorano p157; Jeff Pachoud
p166-167; Keystone-France p69, p124-125; Lars
Ronbog p169; Lionel Bonaventure p177; Michael
Steele p173, p176 bottom; Mike Powell p170 top;
Pascal Rondeau p155; Patrick Hertzog p12-13;

Patrick Kovarik p161; Photo 12 p31; Popperfoto
p26, p27, p36 right, p102 top, p200-201; Print
Collector p16, p46 top; Richard Schroeder p145;
Roger Viollet p45, p47 left, p47 right, p84, p88,
p89; Science & Society Picture Library p17, p43;
STF p70; Topical Press Agency p9; Ullstein Bild
p87, p137, p153; Universal Images Group p37

Courtesy of Herbie Sykes p98, p99

Courtesy of the estate of Marguerite Wilson
p77, p79

Offside: Archivio Farabola p51; L'Equipe p10,
p41, p55, p56 bottom, p56 top, p57, p58-59,
p60 bottom, p60 top, p61 top, p63, p64 bottom,
p64 top, p65, p71, p74 bottom, p74 top, p75,
p82, p105, p110, p111, p115, p127, p134, p135
top; p138, p139, p151, p154, p158, p198, p199,
p207, p208; Presse Sports p61 bottom, p113,
p114; p135 bottom

REX Shutterstock: p149; Canadian Press p193;
John Pierce Owner PhotoSport Int p109, p141,
p142; Photosport International p133, p150

Sporting Cyclist, Time Inc p25

Topfoto p40, p78

Acknowledgements

I'd like to thank my brilliant commissioning
editor Zena Alkayat for taking my vague idea
and helping to turn it into a beautiful book.
Thanks too to Anna Watson for her help with
picture research, Glenn Howard for his striking
design, Vanessa Bird, Laura Nicholson and
Isabel Otter-Barry Ross.

Robert Millar of Scotland
on a solo breakaway up
the Col de la Bonette in
the 1993 Tour de France.
It was a heroically foolhardy
move: he became the
second man to win that
climb but finished the
stage seventh

Henri Colle and Charles
Parel celebrate the
relationship between beer
and bikes in Dalstein during
the 1921 Tour de France.
What professional cyclist
today wouldn't get a pang
of jealousy from looking
at this?